Milk for Babes, Strong Meat for Grown-Ups

MILK FOR BABES, STRONG MEAT FOR GROWN-UPS

Addressing Everyday Challenges from a Biblical Perspective

RAUL N. WALLACE

XULON PRESS

Xulon Press
2301 Lucien Way #415
Maitland, FL 32751
407.339.4217
www.xulonpress.com

Paperback ISBN-13: 978-1-6628-1043-5

Ebook ISBN-13: 978-1-6628-1044-2

This book is dedicated to the spiritual milk drinkers and meat eaters. Yes, you who will read and feast from the table that is spread herein. You who crave the milk and meat from the Living Word will not be denied or disappointed. It is to you, with intense desire, I wish to devote this writing.

Whether you are a babe in Christ, a preteen, adolescent, young adult, or a fully grown grown-up in the Christian faith, I have diligently applied myself in this work to ensure you are not left wanting. I am confident that by the time you are finished reading this book, you will no longer be athirst or famished. I assure you quite the opposite will occur. Your thirst will be quenched and your appetite fully satisfied. You may not be able to drink or eat all of what is served, but I cordially invite you to take, drink, and eat all you can, to your heart's content. Leave the rest to your fellow readers who are capable of managing all that's left. Sufficient spiritual nourishment lies within to serve and satisfy everyone's thirst and hunger.

As you feast from these pages, may you be encouraged and inspired to progress in your spiritual growth and maturity along the developmental spectrum; advancing from newborn babes desiring pure milk to fully grown grown-ups craving strong meat.

Come along. Help yourself. Drink and eat. The table is spread.

Contents

Acknowledgments. ix

Foreword. xi

Preface. xiii

Introduction. xv

Milk and Honey 1

Miracles. 1

What Emboldens. 3

Tired 4

Six of Fifteen. 5

Beyond the Sky. 6

Starved 7

Coward 9

Up Early 11

Funeral Procession 12

GOAT 13

Walk and Chew. 14

Gone 16

You Haven't 17

I Care. 18

Say It Ain't So. 19

This and That 20

I See You. 22

Private Public 23

Here a Little, There a Little. . 25

The Promise 26

Insufficient 27

Marked Man 28

Theories and Conspiracies . . 29

Not Yet 31

Ponytail. 32

How Dare You?. 33

Home. 34

Mad Scientist 36

Closer 37

Stop. 38

Pray. 40

Not So Fast 41

Grand Slam 42

Bumper Stickers 45

Poisoned Pill. 46

Expand 48

Why. 48

The Great Escape 49

Heads-Up 54

Deafening Silence. 54

Strike a Balance 55

Slip Showing. 57

Give Back 59

There's Room 60

Overconfidence. 61

Emergencies 62

Slow Down 64

Honestly 65

Backward and Forward. 66

All for One 68

Doesn't Seem Fair. 69

Bald-Faced Liar 72

Station Identification. 73

Gargantuan Nerve. 74

Dead End. 76

Giving Up 77
Winners and Champions 79
Help's on the Way 80
Rising Up 82
Drink Up 83
Keep It Moving 84
End It 86
Synchronized 87
Final Result 88
Rest and Recuperate 90
All In 91
Come This Far 92
Middle of the Road 93
Care Enough 95
Coming or Going 97
Stop, Look, Listen 97
This or That 98
Positive and Negative 99
Hammer and Nails 100
Stand Your Ground 101
Wrong, Right 102
Enough 102
That One 103
Doing Great 104
Deeper, Higher 105
Ups and Downs 105
Snake 106
Fight 107
Without 107
No Eraser 108
Best and Worse 110
Commonality 111

Look 112
Speak 113
Not Alone 114
Brave 114
Certitude 116
No Turning Back 116
Hardest Fights 117
A Little 118
Nothing 119
Gehenna 119
Tactical 120
Brighter Days 121
Sssstart 122
Listen 123
Opposites 123
Truth and Lies 124
Do and Say 125
Blessed 126
Sides 127
Choices 131
Adversities 132
Worrisome 137
Dominate 138
First Things First 139
Flat Tires 141
Get Dressed 143
Nearly Impossible 145
What's Cooking? 147
What's Going On? 149

Conclusion 153
About The Author 157

Acknowledgments

First and foremost, all thanks, praise, and glory belong to our triune God, who brought to life the Holy Scriptures within my human spirit.

Thanks to my lovely wife, Juanetta, for the many years of support and encouragement to become an author. She would not relent until this work was finished. I would not have followed through with this endeavor had it not been for her cheering me on.

My overwhelming gratitude goes out to Reverend Doctor Otis T. McMillan and Pastor Vertell T. Godbolt for their thorough review and thoughtful input, which contributed tremendously to the completion of this book.

Thanks to One Flesh Photography, the most attentive perfectionist of photographers I had ever encountered.

Last but not the least of all, thanks to my Salem author team for their tireless efforts from conception to completion of this writing project.

Foreword

M*ilk for Babes, Strong Meat for Grown-Ups* by Raul N. Wallace is a standing invitation to all—an invitation to come and dine. Everyone can approach, take, eat, and drink freely to their heart's content. Raul presents these ideas and Scriptures as a sage of old. This book reminds me of the way in which King Solomon of old, God's preacher and prophet, presented the book of Proverbs.

This book is full of witty sayings and thought-provoking statements that challenge the reader to stop, meditate, and deeply consider before moving on. The wonderful love of God, forgiveness, and care toward His children is shared in a discovery style. The sum total and effect of the Scriptures presented are followed by brief statements that partly contain doctrine and partly manners, but always include exhortations. The author's writing is full of grave declarations and deep mysteries that lure the reader into giving diligent attention to what follows next. Each subject opens and closes with a precious jewel that I believe readers will find useful on their life's journey.

I strongly believe each of us will be thoroughly challenged and moved to reexamine ourselves as we respond to the provocative questions at the end of each segment. The life's experiences the author cites in this literature are both powerful and relevant to each of us on our spiritual journeys. As Raul Wallace states, "Despite all that is already behind us, we have really just begun. We cannot afford to rest on our laurels. The death of one thing only precedes the resurrection of another." What a stimulating bit of reading.

Reverend Doctor Otis T. McMillan
Executive Director of the Bureau of Church
Growth and Development
The African Methodist Episcopal Zion Church
Charlotte, North Carolina

Preface

Milk is considered a necessity for newborn babies, but solid food belongs to fully mature adults (Heb. 5:12–14). Both milk and solid foods are essentials for the proper growth and development from infancy to adulthood. With that, there is only one major distinction I will make here: milk is for babes; strong meat is for grown-ups.

The instances you will encounter in this writing are not meant to be interpreted as my personal life experiences. Rather, they were spontaneously written as the Holy Spirit spoke these inspirational words into my spirit, which led me to the Scriptures to discover the light they shone on them.

Within these pages, you will find very little, if any, commentaries on the Scriptures themselves. My approach in tackling this endeavor was simply to hold up life's experiences and challenges to the light of God's Word for careful examination to discern a clearer picture of the whole matter. More directly, what you will find are synopses of a plurality of life's ups and downs, highs and lows, ins and outs, followed by the Word of God concerning the situations. I intentionally avoided inclinations to further elaborate on each circumstance on account of the fact that what God's Word has to say about the matters far outweighs the matters themselves.

For brevity and clarity's sake, Scriptures presented are given in an abbreviated form so to save both time and space. For this purpose I strongly suggest you read with your Bible close at hand. You may need to refer to it often so you can better capture the entire context from which particular Scriptures are taken.

No matter where you fall along the spectrum of your spiritual journey, you will discover someone walking along beside you, holding your hand, whispering deep within, letting you know you're not alone, and lighting your path through the darkness. If you are a babe in Christ, you will find pure milk. Have a drink and be quenched. If you are a grown-up, you will find strong meat. Take a bite and be filled.

Finally, we arrive at certain resolve that lifts us up and sends us on our merry way to meet the next challenge. After reading each synopsis, I encourage you to take a few moments to pause, listen intently to the words of your inner voice, and then reflect on your own personal life experiences and challenges before moving on to the next synopsis.

You may never have personally encountered any of the experiences and challenges presented in this book, but I am certain if you have lived at all, you have had some life oppositions closely related to those enclosed within these pages. Nevertheless, I believe this book will be a tremendous blessing to you, regardless of your current locale along life's journey. Whether or not this blesses you, I humbly ask that you please consider sharing it with someone else whose life may very well be positively affected by it.

Introduction

M ilk is for babes; strong meat belongs to grown-ups. What business have grown-ups with breasts? Come on, now; it's time-out for that. The apostle Peter wrote in 1 Peter 2:2, "Now, like infants at the breast, drink deep of God's pure kindness. Then you'll grow up mature and whole in God" (MSG). Then the writer of the Book of Hebrews upbraided the saints in Hebrews 5:12–14, "You have been believers so long now that you ought to be teaching others. Instead, you need someone to teach you again the basic things about God's Word. You are like babies who need milk and cannot eat solid food. (13) For someone who lives on milk is still an infant and doesn't know how to do what is right. (14) Solid food is for those who are mature, who through training have the skill to recognize the difference between right and wrong" (NLT).

Apostle Paul writes in 1 Corinthians 13:11, "When I was a child, I spoke as a child, I understood as a child, I thought as a child; but when I became a man, I put away childish things" (NKJV). Babes drinking milk from the bottle is both expected and appropriate, but to discover the same of those in adulthood is concerning and abnormal. That ought not to be. Although the milk of God's Word benefits adults as much as it does babes, grown-ups cannot be sustained by milk alone. The strong meat of the Word of God is what fits the bill for the spiritually mature.

The table is spread, the meal is prepared, and the invitation is extended to all in Revelation 22:17, "And the Spirit and the bride say, 'Come!' And let him who hears say, 'Come!' And let him who thirsts come. Whoever desires, let him take the water of life freely" (NKJV). It is a standing invitation to all, from those still in their infant stages to those who are well into adulthood. Each one can approach, take, eat, and drink freely to his heart's content, but it is long past time now for grown-ups to have been weaned off the bottle. It is high time for adults to sink their teeth into solid food and leave milk drinking to the babes.

The table is spread and the feast is prepared. Come one and all, babes and grown-ups alike. Let us eat and drink together. Bon appétit.

Milk and Honey

Milk and honey is a go-to drink mixture of choice. But what's up with the herd of cows and swarm of bees? Oh, I get it: cows are the source of milk and bees are the source of honey. So you care only for the milk and honey? Have a drink or take a bite:

> Exodus 3:8—"And now I have come down to help them, pry them loose from the grip of Egypt, get them out of that country and bring them to a good land with wide-open spaces, a land lush with milk and honey…" (MSG).

> Deuteronomy 32:13, 14—"And he made him to suck honey out of the rock, and oil out of the flinty rock; (14) butter of kine, and milk of sheep..."

Milk does not miraculously appear in refrigerated bottles, nor honey in jars stocked on shelves. Someone has to assume the responsibility of transforming them from one form to the other. With that, it is time to get busy milking your cows and tending your hives. Hurry on, now. Milk your cows and harvest your honey. Yes, go on, work it out. Expect no handouts.

Pause—Listen—Reflect

* * * * * * * * *

Miracles

I finally caught up with the crippled man who ran past me and asked him, "What happened?" He responded, "Ask the blind man; he saw everything." So I asked the blind man, "What happened?" He retorted, "Ask the deaf man; he heard it all." So I asked the deaf man, "What happened?" He replied, "Ask the mute; he'll tell you all you care to know." The mute couldn't get one word out before a dead man rose up and hollered at the top of his lungs, "I once was dead but now I'm alive forevermore." To that, the crippled man shouted, "I can walk." The blind man yelled, "I can see." The deaf man cried out, "And I can hear." "That's nothing," said the mute. "Listen to this: I can speak and sing again." Jesus must be near. Have a drink or take a bite:

> Isaiah 35:5, 6—"The eyes of the blind shall be opened, and the ears of the deaf shall be unstopped. (6) Then shall the lame *man* leap as an hart, and the tongue of the dumb sing..."

> Matthew 4:23—"And Jesus went about all Galilee... and healing all manner of sickness and all manner of disease among the people."

> Matthew 11:4, 5—"Jesus answered and said unto them, Go and shew John again those things which ye do hear and see: (5) The blind receive their sight, and the lame walk, the lepers are cleansed, and the deaf hear, the dead are raised up..."

> Luke 4:18—"The Spirit of the Lord is upon me, for he has anointed me to bring Good News to the poor. He has sent me to proclaim that captives will be released, that the blind will see, that the oppressed will be set free" (NLT).

> Acts 10:38—"God anointed Jesus of Nazareth with the Holy Ghost and with power: who went about doing good, and healing all that were oppressed of the devil; for God was with him."

Jesus is still working miracles. John Newton captured it right: "Amazing grace, how sweet the sound that saved a wretch like me. I once was lost, but now I'm found, was blind, but now I see."

Pause—Listen—Reflect

* * * * * * * * *

What Emboldens

What makes them think they can lead the way? They haven't even had a few good years of life's experiences yet! Whatever got into them at such a tender age? How audacious of them. They've got the nerve. Have a drink or take a bite:

> Isaiah 11:6, 8—"The wolf also shall dwell with the lamb, and the leopard shall lie down with the kid; and the calf and the young lion and the fatling together; and a little child shall lead them... (8) And the sucking child shall play on the hole of the asp, and the weaned child shall put his hand on the cockatrice's den."

> Matthew 18:3–5—"Verily I say unto you, Except ye be converted, and become as little children, ye shall not enter into the kingdom of heaven. (4) Whosoever therefore shall humble himself as this little child, the same is greatest in the kingdom of heaven. (5) And whoso shall receive one such little child in my name receiveth me."

> Luke 18:16, 17—"Suffer little children to come unto me, and forbid them not: for of such is the kingdom of God. (17) Verily I say unto you, Whosoever shall not receive the kingdom of God as a little child shall in no wise enter therein."

What did you say? Really? Do you think that is what emboldens them? Oh, Jesus, please take the wheel. Then again, nothing compares to a childlike faith. That just might be the solution to all our troubles.

Pause—Listen—Reflect

* * * * * * * *

Tired

Left stranded, way out in the middle of the deep, dark blue sea, without a vessel to get back ashore, not even a life vest to hang on to, just about all out of breath, wickedly tired as all get-out; nevertheless, refuse to go down in a watery grave. Kick in the teeth, the very notion of being pinned to a mat. No, not here! Not now! Not while you can still catch a glimpse of the breaking of dawn out on the horizon. Have a drink or take a bite:

> Genesis 32:24–26—"And Jacob was left alone; and there wrestled a man with him until the breaking of the day. (25) And when he saw that he prevailed not against him, he touched the hollow of his thigh; and the hollow of Jacob's thigh was out of joint, as he wrestled with him. (26) And he said, Let me go, for the day breaketh. And he said, I will not let thee go, except thou bless me."

> Hosea 12:3, 4—"He took his brother by the heel in the womb, and by his strength he had power with God: (4) Yea, he had power over the angel, and prevailed: He wept, and made supplication unto him..."

Never give up. Never give in. Hang on with the tenacity and resolve of a bulldog's grip. Do not let go until He blesses you.

It takes just that kind of determination to swim back to shore. If I made it back (and it wasn't easy), so can you.

Pause—Listen—Reflect

* * * * * * * * *

Six of Fifteen

It is only round six of a fifteen-round match. You have nine whole rounds left to go. So get up and get back in the ring. Summon the fortitude from where it lies. You can still win this fight. Game on! Have a drink or take a bite:

> Isaiah 40:28–31—"Have you never heard? Have you never understood? The Lord is the everlasting God, the Creator of all the earth. He never grows weak or weary. No one can measure the depths of his understanding. (29) He gives power to the weak and strength to the powerless. (30) Even youths will become weak and tired, and young men will fall in exhaustion. (31) But those who trust in the Lord will find new strength. They will soar high on wings like eagles. They will run and not grow weary. They will walk and not faint" (NLT).

> Romans 8:37—"Nay, in all these things we are more than conquerors through him that loved us."

> 1 Corinthians 9:26—"I therefore so run, not as uncertainly; so fight I, not as one that beateth the air..."

> 1 Corinthians 15:57—"But thanks *be* to God, which giveth us the victory through our Lord Jesus Christ."

> 2 Corinthians 2:14—"Now thanks *be* unto God, which always causeth us to triumph in Christ..."

> 1 Timothy 6:12—"Fight the good fight of faith, lay hold on eternal life, whereunto thou art also called, and hast professed a good profession before many witnesses."

> 1 John 5:4—"For whatsoever is born of God overcometh the world: and this is the victory that overcometh the world, *even* our faith."

There are winners; then there are losers. Winners never lose and losers never win. There is the thrill of victory and the agony of defeat. Winners take all. Losers get absolutely nada. You are a winner. Never accept defeat. So revel in the thrill but abhor defeat. Remember, winners take all.

Pause—Listen—Reflect

* * * * * * * * *

Beyond the Sky

Beyond the sky is your limit. So take the brakes off. You are not even halfway there yet, but it's still well within your reach. Have a drink or take a bite:

> Philippians 4:13—"I can do all things through Christ which strengtheneth me."

Stop restricting the God within you. It is in Him you live, move, and have your being (Acts 17:28).

Pause—Listen—Reflect

* * * * * * * *

Starved

No matter how love-starved, relationship-starved, companion-ship-starved, or affection-starved you are, you are heaps better off being all alone, wishing you had somebody, than to be stuck with somebody, wishing you were all alone. I do not mean to make light of your starvation. It isn't that it does not matter. It really and truly does matter. But you are still loads better off being all alone, wishing you had someone, than to be stuck with that someone, wishing you were all alone. I do realize this perspective seems disconnected and callous, but know this is not the end of your line. There is much better in store for you. First up, have a drink or take a bite:

> Isaiah 54:5–7—"For thy Maker is thine husband; the Lord of hosts is his name; and thy Redeemer the Holy One of Israel; the God of the whole earth shall he be called. (6) For the Lord hath called thee as a woman forsaken and grieved in spirit, and a wife of youth, when thou wast refused, saith thy God. (7) For a small moment have I forsaken thee; but with great mercies will I gather thee."

> Isaiah 62:5—"For as a young man marrieth a virgin, so shall thy sons marry thee: And as the bridegroom rejoiceth over the bride, so shall thy God rejoice over thee."

Jeremiah 3:1, 14—"They say, If a man put away his wife, and she go from him, and become another man's, shall he return unto her again?... (14) Turn, O backsliding children, saith the Lord; for I am married unto you..."

Jeremiah 31:3—"Yea, I have loved thee with an everlasting love: Therefore with lovingkindness have I drawn thee."

Lamentations 1:2—"She weepeth sore in the night, and her tears are on her cheeks: Among all her lovers she hath none to comfort her: All her friends have dealt treacherously with her, they are become her enemies."

Ezekiel 16:8—"Now when I passed by thee, and looked upon thee, behold, thy time was the time of love; and I spread my skirt over thee, and covered thy nakedness: yea, I sware unto thee, and entered into a covenant with thee, saith the Lord God, and thou becamest mine."

Hosea 2:7, 16, 19, 20—And she shall follow after her lovers, but she shall not overtake them; and she shall seek them, but shall not find them: Then shall she say, I will go and return to my first husband; for then was it better with me than now... (16) And it shall be at that day, saith the Lord, that thou shalt call me Ishi... (19) And I will betroth thee unto me for ever; Yea, I will betroth thee unto me in righteousness, and in judgment, and in lovingkindness, and in mercies. (20) I will even betroth thee unto me in faithfulness..."

John 15:9–11—"As the Father hath loved me, so have I loved you: continue ye in my love. (10) If

ye keep my commandments, ye shall abide in my
love; even as I have kept my Father's commandments, and abide in his love. (11) These things
have I spoken unto you, that my joy might remain
in you, and that your joy might be full."

Agape love! After all this, who needs anything more? It simply
gets no better than this. I did begin with "First up," but there's just
no need for a "Second up." He is more to be desired than fine gold
and sweeter than honey and the honeycomb (Ps. 19:10).

Pause—Listen—Reflect

* * * * * * * * *

Coward

What a coward. Hypocrite! That's worse than throwing rocks and
hiding your hands. That is totally despicable. Have a drink or
take a bite:

1 Kings 3:19–22—"And this woman's child died
in the night; because she overlaid it. (20) And she
arose at midnight, and took my son from beside
me, while thine handmaid slept, and laid it in her
bosom, and laid her dead child in my bosom. (21)
And when I rose in the morning to give my child
suck, behold, it was dead: but when I had considered it in the morning, behold, it was not my
son, which I did bear. (22) And the other woman
said, Nay; but the living *is* my son, and the dead
is thy son."

Matthew 13:25–30—"But while men slept, his
enemy came and sowed tares among the wheat,
and went his way. (26) But when the blade was

sprung up, and brought forth fruit, then appeared the tares also. (27) So the servants of the house-holder came and said unto him, Sir, didst not thou sow good seed in thy field? from whence then hath it tares? (28) He said unto them, An enemy hath done this. The servants said unto him, Wilt thou then that we go and gather them up? (29) But he said, Nay; lest while ye gather up the tares, ye root up also the wheat with them. (30) Let both grow together until the harvest: and in the time of har-vest I will say to the reapers, Gather ye together first the tares, and bind them in bundles to burn them: but gather the wheat into my barn."

Luke 11:39, 46, 52—"Now do ye Pharisees make clean the outside of the cup and the platter; but your inward part is full of ravening and wicked-ness... (46) Woe unto you also, *ye* lawyers! for ye lade men with burdens grievous to be borne, and ye yourselves touch not the burdens with one of your fingers... (52) Woe unto you, lawyers! for ye have taken away the key of knowledge: ye entered not in yourselves, and them that were entering in ye hindered."

Luke 12:1–3—"Beware ye of the leaven of the Pharisees, which is hypocrisy. (2) For there is nothing covered, that shall not be revealed; neither hid, that shall not be known. (3) Therefore whatso-ever ye have spoken in darkness shall be heard in the light; and that which ye have spoken in the ear in closets shall be proclaimed upon the housetops."

Be careful, be careful, be careful what you throw at others when you live in a glass house yourself. The stones you throw, watch out; they travel in circles and come back around again. It's called a boomerang, coming right back atcha, baby. You never walk away unscathed. You will always pay the piper.

Pause—Listen—Reflect

* * * * * * * *

Up Early

Everyone should have been up early in the morning waiting expectantly for it, but unfortunately, it seems nobody was. I do not understand why because, without fail, early every morning, the beautiful sunrise always shines brightly over the horizon, just like clockwork. I guess that morning's glorious Son-rise outshone the usual daily sunrise. Nobody expected that, although they should have. He had warned of the rising Son. Nonetheless, everyone was caught off guard. They should not have been, though. Have a drink or take a bite:

> Psalm 16:9, 10—"Therefore my heart is glad, and my glory rejoiceth: My flesh also shall rest in hope. (10) For thou wilt not leave my soul in hell; neither wilt thou suffer thine Holy One to see corruption."

> Matthew 12:40—"For as Jonas was three days and three nights in the whale's belly; so shall the Son of man be three days and three nights in the heart of the earth."

> Matthew 27:63—"Sir, we remember what that deceiver once said while he was still alive: After three days I will rise from the dead."

The Son is up. Yes, and has been up and shining brightly too. He is giving light to everyone. Can't you see?

Pause—Listen—Reflect

* * * * * * * * *

Funeral Procession

You say you died, and long ago too. So you say. That's great. Now tell me: how long is your funeral procession going to last? The average only lasts but a short while. Have a drink or take a bite:

> Romans 6:1, 2, 11–14—"What shall we say then? Shall we continue in sin, that grace may abound? (2) God forbid. How shall we, that are dead to sin, live any longer therein?... (11) Likewise reckon ye also yourselves to be dead indeed unto sin, but alive unto God through Jesus Christ our Lord. (12) Let not sin therefore reign in your mortal body, that ye should obey it in the lusts thereof. (13) Neither yield ye your members *as* instruments of unrighteousness unto sin: but yield yourselves unto God, as those that are alive from the dead, and your members *as* instruments of righteousness unto God. (14) For sin shall not have dominion over you: for ye are not under the law, but under grace."

> Romans 7:4, 6—"Wherefore, my brethren, ye also are become dead to the law by the body of Christ; that ye should be married to another, *even* to him who is raised from the dead, that we should bring forth fruit unto God... (6) But now we are delivered from the law, that being dead wherein we were held; that we should serve in newness of spirit, and not *in* the oldness of the letter."

> Romans 8:2—"For the law of the Spirit of life in Christ Jesus hath made me free from the law of sin and death."

> Colossians 3:9, 10—"Lie not one to another, seeing that ye have put off the old man with his deeds; (10) and have put on the new *man*, which is renewed in knowledge after the image of him that created him..."

> Galatians 2:19, 20—"For I through the law am dead to the law, that I might live unto God. (20) I am crucified with Christ: nevertheless I live; yet not I, but Christ liveth in me: and the life which I now live in the flesh I live by the faith of the Son of God, who loved me, and gave himself for me."

By now you should have been experiencing the resurrected life, not still having a funeral procession. Get on with it. No one likes funerals, especially lengthy ones.

Pause—Listen—Reflect

* * * * * * * *

GOAT

Hercules, Superman, Wonder Woman, the Incredible Hulk, Iron Man, Captain America, Captain Marvel—all very great superheroes in their own right. Be that as it may, none are the least bit so stupendous as the greatest of all. And I'm not referring to Cassius Marcellus Clay, either. He isn't even in a comparable category. Have a drink or take a bite:

> Genesis 1:2, 3—"And the earth was without form, and void; and darkness *was* upon the face of the

deep. And the Spirit of God moved upon the face of the waters. (3) And God said, Let there be light: and there was light."

Job 26:8, 10, 12–14—"He bindeth up the waters in his thick clouds; And the cloud is not rent under them... (10) He hath compassed the waters with bounds, until the day and night come to an end... (12) He divideth the sea with his power, and by his understanding he smiteth through the proud. (13) By his spirit he hath garnished the heavens; His hand hath formed the crooked serpent. (14) Lo, these *are* parts of his ways: But how little a portion is heard of him? But the thunder of his power who can understand?"

Daniel 4:35—"And he doeth according to his will in the army of heaven, and *among* the inhabitants of the earth: and none can stay his hand, or say unto him, What doest thou?"

Indeed, He is the superhero of superheroes. He is the renowned undisputed heavyweight champion of champions, hands down. He is the greatest of all times. Yes, Jesus is the true and original GOAT.

Pause—Listen—Reflect

* * * * * * * * *

Walk and Chew

Surely we can walk and chew gum at the same time. Keep an eye on that over there while handling this over here. As strange as it may seem to some, you can even keep your eyes wide open while you pray. Not only that, double-dealing is also allowed here too. It isn't all dishonesty, either. Have a drink or take a bite:

Nehemiah 4:9, 16–18—"Nevertheless we made our prayer unto our God, and set a watch against them day and night... (16) And it came to pass from that time forth, that the half of my servants wrought in the work, and the other half of them held both the spears, the shields, and the bows, and the habergeons... (17) They which builded on the wall, and they that bare burdens, with those that laded, every one with one of his hands wrought in the work, and with the other hand held a weapon. (18) For the builders, every one had his sword girded by his side, and so builded..."

Matthew 26:41—"Watch and pray, that ye enter not into temptation: the spirit indeed is willing, but the flesh is weak."

Mark 13:33—"Take ye heed, watch and pray: for ye know not when the time is."

1 Peter 5:8—"Be sober, be vigilant; because your adversary the devil, as a roaring lion, walketh about, seeking whom he may devour."

Yes, we have faith. Yes, we trust God. Yes, we believe His Word. But that does not mean we behave ourselves foolishly. There is an enemy out there on the prowl, and he doesn't care one iota what you believe. He wouldn't offer you two bits for your faith and trust in God. Take necessary precautions and have safety measures in place. Watch and pray. When you are done with that, then pray and watch. We cannot afford to be running as a loose cannon.

Pause—Listen—Reflect

* * * * * * * *

Gone

Now you see me. Soon you won't. You will look for me, but I'll be nowhere to be found. I will be gone; gone home. Have a drink or take a bite:

> Matthew 24:31—"And he shall send his angels with a great sound of a trumpet, and they shall gather together his elect from the four winds, from one end of heaven to the other."

> 1 Corinthians 15:51–53—"Behold, I shew you a mystery; we shall not all sleep, but we shall all be changed, (52) in a moment, in the twinkling of an eye, at the last trump: for the trumpet shall sound, and the dead shall be raised incorruptible, and we shall be changed. (53) For this corruptible must put on incorruption, and this mortal must put on immortality."

> Philippians 3:20, 21—"For our conversation is in heaven; from whence also we look for the Saviour, the Lord Jesus Christ: (21) Who shall change our vile body, that it may be fashioned like unto his glorious body, according to the working whereby he is able even to subdue all things unto himself."

> 1 Thessalonians 4:16, 17—For the Lord himself shall descend from heaven with a shout, with the voice of the archangel, and with the trump of God: and the dead in Christ shall rise first: (17) Then we which are alive and remain shall be caught up together with them in the clouds, to meet the Lord in the air: and so shall we ever be with the Lord."

> Hebrews 10:37—"For yet a little while, and he that shall come will come, and will not tarry."

> 1 John 3:2, 3—"Beloved, now are we the sons of
> God, and it doth not yet appear what we shall be:
> but we know that, when he shall appear, we shall
> be like him; for we shall see him as he is. (3) And
> every man that hath this hope in him purifieth him-
> self, even as he is pure."

So go ahead, take a good look. Get an eyeful. Soon you will be
searching for me and I'll be gone. I am not just shooting the breeze,
either. I live my life each day with this great expectation. This is an
eternal promise from my Heavenly Father. Do you want to come
along? You can. He has given you the selfsame eternal promise.

Pause—Listen—Reflect

* * * * * * * *

You Haven't

Have you seen Him? Really? Are you sure you have ever seen
Him? I find it hard to believe that. No, I do not believe you have.
You never have. No, never. Allow me to enlighten you on what
you might have seen. Have a drink or take a bite:

> John 1:14, 18—"And the Word was made flesh,
> and dwelt among us, (and we beheld his glory, the
> glory as of the only begotten of the Father,) full of
> grace and truth... (18) No man hath seen God at
> any time; the only begotten Son, which is in the
> bosom of the Father, he hath declared him."

> Exodus 33:20—"Thou canst not see my face: for
> there shall no man see me, and live."

> 1 Timothy 6:15, 16—"Which in his times he shall
> shew, who is the blessed and only Potentate, the

King of kings, and Lord of lords; (16) who only hath immortality, dwelling in the light which no man can approach unto; whom no man hath seen, nor can see..."

Here is what you saw: you beheld what He had on, not who He is. He is the I Am. You have just been attentive to a semblance of what He wore. You would never be able to handle His pure, unfiltered presence. You have only recognized Him through His varied manifestations wherein He cloaked Himself! He is Spirit. He is Light. He is Love. He is Wisdom. He is Power. He is Holy. He is Truth. He just is! No one can ever handle Him in all of His glory and splendor. You will have to wait for your immortal, incorruptible body for that.

Pause—Listen—Reflect

* * * * * * * * *

I Care

Some may say, "We really do not care if you are offended. Nor do we give a hoot how you feel." Seriously, they really and truly mean it too. But before I go there, first let's consider this. Have a drink or take a bite:

John 1:17—"For the law was given by Moses, but grace and truth came by Jesus Christ."

John 8:32—"And ye shall know the truth, and the truth shall make you free."

John 13:34, 35—"A new commandment I give unto you, that ye love one another; as I have loved you, that ye also love one another. (35) By this shall all men know that ye are my disciples, if ye have love one to another."

Romans 12:10—"Be kindly affectioned one to another with brotherly love; in honour preferring one another..."

1 Thessalonians 4:9—"But as touching brotherly love ye need not that I write unto you: for ye yourselves are taught of God to love one another."

Hebrews 13:1—"Let brotherly love continue."

Let me be the first to confess: I am deeply concerned whenever it's brought to my attention that I have offended someone. Really, I do sincerely care about one's well-being after I have committed an act of offense, even more so when it's having to do with the things of God. It's just that I really and truly do much, much more seriously care about one coming face-to-face with the undiluted truth. What I am confident of is this: it is the truth that makes you free (Jn. 8:32). God be my witness, I never set out to offend, but truth is paramount. So please, please do not be offended. That is never my intent.

Pause—Listen—Reflect

* * * * * * * *

Say It Ain't So

Surely this cannot still be just the beginning. It seems to me we have been at this since ages past. I mean since the beginning of time. Please say it isn't so. Have a drink or take a bite:

19

Psalm 90:4—"For a thousand years in thy sight are but as yesterday when it is past, and as a watch in the night."

2 Peter 3:8—"But, beloved, be not ignorant of this one thing, that one day is with the Lord as a thousand years, and a thousand years as one day."

So what is this saying to you? What is it telling of? Namely this: get back in the saddle. Yes, right back up in there. We still have a long way to go yet. We are not quite done here. Keep in mind: we are on His time, not ours. His grace is sufficient for us (2 Cor. 12:9).

Pause—Listen—Reflect

* * * * * * * *

This and That

That is just wonderful. Thank God we are finally finished with that. All done! Finito! But do not fall asleep just yet. Unrecline your chair. Let's not be mistaken—although *that* is finished, *this* has just begun. Have a drink or take a bite:

Isaiah 43:18, 19—"Remember ye not the former things, neither consider the things of old. (19) Behold, I will do a new thing; now it shall spring forth; shall ye not know it? I will even make a way in the wilderness, and rivers in the desert."

Romans 6:4—"Therefore we are buried with him by baptism into death: that like as Christ was raised up from the dead by the glory of the Father, even so we also should walk in newness of life."

1 Corinthians 13:11—When I was a child, I spake as a child, I understood as a child, I thought as a child: but when I became a man, I put away childish things."

2 Corinthians 5:17—"Therefore if any man be in Christ, he is a new creature: old things are passed away; behold, all things are become new."

Ephesians 4:22–24—"That ye put off concerning the former conversation the old man, which is corrupt according to the deceitful lusts; (23) and be renewed in the spirit of your mind; (24) and that ye put on the new man, which after God is created in righteousness and true holiness ..."

Colossians 3:3, 5, 7–10—"For ye are dead, and your life is hid with Christ in God... (5) Mortify therefore your members which are upon the earth... (7) In the which ye also walked some time, when ye lived in them. (8) But now ye also put off all these. (9) ...seeing that ye have put off the old man with his deeds; (10) And have put on the new man, which is renewed in knowledge after the image of him that created him."

Despite all that is already behind us, we have really just begun. We cannot afford to rest on our laurels. The death of one thing only precedes the resurrection of another.

Pause—Listen—Reflect

* * * * * * * *

I See You

I see you sitting there behind that wide smile of yours doing every-thing in your power, earnestly toiling to keep your head above water. I see you laboring diligently, holding at bay the threat-ening possibility of drowning, going under for the very last time; at all cost, sparing nothing; rooting up every stop just to buy the tiniest bit more time. I see you refusing to willingly go into default. I even smell, permeating the air, the stench of burning rubber from the skid marks of you digging in. You don't have to tell me. Believe me when I tell you, I know. Know what? There is nothing easy or simple about remaining afloat. Have a drink or take a bite:

> Psalm 27:13—"I had fainted, unless I had believed to see the goodness of the Lord in the land of the living."

> 1 Corinthians 16:13—"Watch ye, stand fast in the faith, quit you like men, be strong."

> Ephesians 6:13–18—"Wherefore take unto you the whole armour of God, that ye may be able to withstand in the evil day, and having done all, to stand. (14) Stand therefore, having your loins girt about with truth, and having on the breastplate of righteousness; (15) And your feet shod with the preparation of the gospel of peace; (16) Above all, taking the shield of faith, wherewith ye shall be able to quench all the fiery darts of the wicked. (17) And take the helmet of salvation, and the sword of the Spirit, which is the word of God: (18) Praying always with all prayer and supplication in the Spirit, and watching thereunto with all persever-ance and supplication for all saints."

> 1 Thessalonians 3:7, 8—"Therefore, brethren, we were comforted over you in all our affliction and

distress by your faith: (8) For now we live, if ye
stand fast in the Lord."

Keep fighting. Fight like your survival depends on it because it
does. Keep pounding away. Pound away at life as if your destination is conditioned by it. Yes, because it does. An army of
survivors is cheering you on. They have pummeled through far
worse struggles and overcame. So will you. Only never give up.
Never give in.

Pause—Listen—Reflect

* * * * * * * * *

Private Public

Have you ever experienced a private and humiliating moment in a
public setting? Maybe you have, but I promise you—I guarantee
you—you have never, ever encountered anything the likes of these
jaw-dropping moments. Have a drink or take a bite:

> Job 16:10, 11—"They have gaped upon me with
> their mouth; they have smitten me upon the cheek
> reproachfully; they have gathered themselves
> together against me. (11) God hath delivered me
> to the ungodly, and turned me over into the hands
> of the wicked."

> Isaiah 50:6, 7—"I gave my back to the smiters, and
> my cheeks to them that plucked off the hair: I hid
> not my face from shame and spitting. (7) For the
> Lord God will help me; therefore shall I not be con-
> founded: Therefore have I set my face like a flint."

> Lamentations 3:30–32—"He giveth his cheek to
> him that smiteth him: he is filled full with reproach.

(31) For the Lord will not cast off for ever: (32) But though he cause grief, yet will he have compassion according to the multitude of his mercies."

Matthew 27:27–31—"Then the soldiers of the governor took Jesus into the common hall, and gathered unto him the whole band of soldiers. (28) And they stripped him, and put on him a scarlet robe. (29) And when they had platted a crown of thorns, they put it upon his head, and a reed in his right hand: and they bowed the knee before him, and mocked him, saying, Hail, King of the Jews! (30) And they spit upon him, and took the reed, and smote him on the head. (31) And after that they had mocked him, they took the robe off from him, and put his own raiment on him, and led him away to crucify him."

Mark 14:65—"And some began to spit on him, and to cover his face, and to buffet him, and to say unto him, Prophesy: and the servants did strike him with the palms of their hands."

Whatever we have had to put up with, no matter how perverse, it all pales—hands down—in comparison to what our Savior endured. All at His expense, yet for our gain. He never shunned, not even for one moment, the private yet public humiliating moments. He underwent it all for you and for me. How can we ever repay, or at least, demonstrate our gratitude to Him after such an act as that? With an everlasting dedication and lifelong commitment, I'd proffer.

Pause—Listen—Reflect

* * * * * * * * *

Here a Little, There a Little

Little by little. Bit by bit. Easy as you go. Beware, things begin adding up really fast. Before you realize it, everything becomes unhinged. Way out of control, then they totally slip out from under you. Stay steady. Take it slow. Calculate every step. Have a drink or take a bite:

> Proverbs 6:10, 11—"Yet a little sleep, a little slumber, a little folding of the hands to sleep: (11) So shall thy poverty come as one that travelleth, and thy want as an armed man."

> Isaiah 28:10, 13—"For precept must be upon precept, precept upon precept; line upon line, line upon line; here a little, and there a little... (13) But the word of the Lord was unto them Precept upon precept, precept upon precept; Line upon line, line upon line; Here a little, and there a little..."

> Matthew 16:6–8, 11, 12—"Then Jesus said unto them, Take heed and beware of the leaven of the Pharisees and of the Sadducees. (7) And they reasoned among themselves, saying, 'It is because we have taken no bread.' (8) Which when Jesus perceived, he said unto them, 'O ye of little faith, why reason ye among yourselves, because ye have brought no bread?' (11) How is it that ye do not understand that I spake it not to you concerning bread, that ye should beware of the leaven of the Pharisees and of the Sadducees? (12) Then understood they how that he bade them not beware of the leaven of bread, but of the doctrine of the Pharisees and of the Sadducees."

> 1 Corinthians 5:6, 7—"Your glorying is not good. Know ye not that a little leaven leaveneth the whole

lump? (7) Purge out therefore the old leaven, that ye may be a new lump, as ye are unleavened..."

2 Timothy 2:16, 17—"Avoid worthless, foolish talk that only leads to more godless behavior. (17) This kind of talk spreads like cancer..." (NLT).

2 Timothy 3:13—"But evil people and impostors will flourish. They will deceive others and will themselves be deceived" (NLT).

One plus one equals two. It doesn't take too many pluses before stuff really begins adding up. Then before you know it, things become much more than you can handle; way out of your control. Here a little, there a little. It really adds up fast. Watch your step every step of the way. Beware the leaven. It ruins the whole lump.

Pause—Listen—Reflect

* * * * * * * *

The Promise

If you are still lost, it is quite possibly because you are not seeking. You may be out just for a stroll in the park but not seeking. Looking on, yes, but not seeking. Maybe you are only along for the ride but not really searching. Here is a long-standing eternal promise to you. Have a drink or take a bite:

Isaiah 55:6—"Seek ye the Lord while he may be found, call ye upon him while he is near."

Jeremiah 3:14—"Turn, O backsliding children, saith the Lord; for I am married unto you..."

Jeremiah 29:13, 14—"And ye shall seek me, and find me, when ye shall search for me with all your heart. (14) And I will be found of you, saith the Lord: and I will turn away your captivity, and I will gather you from all the nations, and from all the places whither I have driven you, saith the Lord; and I will bring you again into the place whence I caused you to be carried away captive."

Luke 11:9, 10—"Ask, and it shall be given you; seek, and ye shall find; knock, and it shall be opened unto you. (10) For every one that asketh receiveth; and he that seeketh findeth; and to him that knocketh it shall be opened."

Now for the conclusion of the whole matter: this age-old promise still stands. It is a wide-open door of opportunity. What's preventing you from finding your way back home? He remarries backsliders (Jer. 3:14).

Pause—Listen—Reflect

* * * * * * * *

Insufficient

It is not sufficient for us only to be maintaining our grounds. By now, we should be well on our way, gaining ground, turbo-charged. Have a drink or take a bite:

John 16:33—"These things I have spoken unto you, that in me ye might have peace. In the world ye shall have tribulation: but be of good cheer; I have overcome the world."

1 Corinthians 15:57, 58—"But thanks be to God, which giveth us the victory through our Lord Jesus Christ. (58) Therefore, my beloved brethren, be ye stedfast, unmoveable, always abounding in the work of the Lord, forasmuch as ye know that your labour is not in vain in the Lord."

2 Corinthians 2:14, 15—"Now thanks be unto God, which always causeth us to triumph in Christ, and maketh manifest the savour of his knowledge by us in every place. (15) For we are unto God a sweet savour of Christ, in them that are saved, and in them that perish."

1 John 4:4—"Ye are of God, little children, and have overcome them: because greater is he that is in you, than he that is in the world."

1 John 5:4, 5—"For whatsoever is born of God overcometh the world: and this is the victory that overcometh the world, even our faith. (5) Who is he that overcometh the world, but he that believeth that Jesus is the Son of God?"

Do not be caught lagging behind. You are much better than that. So pick up the pace. Go ahead, speed up. Warp speed.

Pause—Listen—Reflect

* * * * * * * * *

Marked Man

Yes, you are a marked man. You have an immense—I mean ginormous—bull's eye right in the center of your back. But, no need to fear. Do not fret yourself. Keep calm. Only keep the faith. Have a drink or take a bite:

> Matthew 26:31, 32—"Then saith Jesus unto them, All ye shall be offended because of me this night: for it is written, I will smite the shepherd, and the sheep of the flock shall be scattered abroad. (32) But after I am risen again, I will go before you into Galilee."

> Luke 22:31, 32—"And the Lord said, Simon, Simon, behold, Satan hath desired to have you, that he may sift you as wheat: (32) But I have prayed for thee, that thy faith fail not: and when thou art converted, strengthen thy brethren."

You are covered and secured in good hands. He's got your back. Yes, just keep the faith.

Pause—Listen—Reflect

* * * * * * * * *

Theories and Conspiracies

There are so many theories going around. It is arduous to decipher which is conspiracy and which is authentically plausible. This one, though, you can bet your bottom dollar. Take it to the bank. This for sure will cash, guaranteed. You can rest assured. Have a drink or take a bite:

> Matthew 24:23–27—"Then if any man shall say unto you, Lo, here is Christ, or there; believe it not. (24) For there shall arise false Christs, and false prophets, and shall shew great signs and wonders; insomuch that, if it were possible, they shall

deceive the very elect. (25) Behold, I have told you before. (26) Wherefore if they shall say unto you, Behold, he is in the desert; go not forth: behold, he is in the secret chambers; believe it not. (27) For as the lightning cometh out of the east, and shineth even unto the west; so shall also the coming of the Son of man be."

Luke 21:8–11, 20, 25–28—"And he said, Take heed that ye be not deceived: for many shall come in my name, saying, I am Christ; and the time draweth near: go ye not therefore after them. (9) But when ye shall hear of wars and commotions, be not terrified: for these things must first come to pass; but the end is not by and by... (10) Nation shall rise against nation, and kingdom against kingdom: (11) And great earthquakes shall be in divers places, and famines, and pestilences; and fearful sights and great signs shall there be from heaven... (20) And when ye shall see Jerusalem compassed with armies, then know that the desolation thereof is nigh... (25) And there shall be signs in the sun, and in the moon, and in the stars; and upon the earth distress of nations, with perplexity; the sea and the waves roaring; (26) Men's hearts failing them for fear, and for looking after those things which are coming on the earth: for the powers of heaven shall be shaken. (27) And then shall they see the Son of man coming in a cloud with power and great glory. (28) And when these things begin to come to pass, then look up, and lift up your heads; for your redemption draweth nigh."

Now this is the gospel truth. Mark these words. There is no conspiracy theory here, only the authentically plausible truth.

Pause—Listen—Reflect

* * * * * * * * *

Not Yet

No, not yet. The end is not yet. It is on its way but not quite here yet. Although it is closer now than it has ever been before. Have a drink or take a bite:

> Matthew 24:3–8—"His disciples came to Him privately and said, 'Tell us, when will all this happen? What sign will signal your return and the end of the world?' (4) Jesus told them, 'Don't let anyone mislead you, (5) for many will come in My name, claiming, "I am the Messiah." They will deceive many. (6) And you will hear of wars and threats of wars, but don't panic. Yes, these things must take place, but the end won't follow immediately. (7) Nation will go to war against nation, and kingdom against kingdom. There will be famines and earthquakes in many parts of the world. (8) But all this is only the first of the birth pains, with more to come'" (NLT).

This was spoken a very long time ago; therefore, we can safely say it must be nearer now than it was then. But we still have some time left. Not as long as before, to be sure. But yes, we have a bit more time left on the clock. So let us get busy doing the work of the Kingdom. There are many who are scared straight, clear out of their minds. They are panicked above, panicked beneath, and all around. Let's share with them the Good News.

Pause—Listen—Reflect

* * * * * * * * *

Ponytail

What are your thoughts on the ponytail? Should we keep the pony and ditch the tail? Or should we leave it in place, just the way it is? Have a drink or take a bite:

> Genesis 21:10–13—"Cast out this bondwoman and her son: for the son of this bondwoman shall not be heir with my son, even with Isaac. (11) And the thing was very grievous in Abraham's sight because of his son. (12) And God said unto Abraham, Let it not be grievous in thy sight because of the lad, and because of thy bondwoman; in all that Sarah hath said unto thee, hearken unto her voice; for in Isaac shall thy seed be called. (13) And also of the son of the bondwoman will I make a nation, because he is thy seed."

> Amos 3:3—"Can two walk together, except they be agreed?"

> Luke 16:13—"No servant can serve two masters: for either he will hate the one, and love the other; or else he will hold to the one, and despise the other. Ye cannot serve God and mammon."

> 1 Corinthians 5:6–8—"Your glorying is not good. Know ye not that a little leaven leaveneth the whole lump? (7) Purge out therefore the old leaven,

that ye may be a new lump, as ye are unleavened. For even Christ our passover is sacrificed for us: (8) Therefore let us keep the feast, not with old leaven, neither with the leaven of malice and wickedness; but with the unleavened bread of sincerity and truth."

Unequivocally, you must choose one over the other. There is just no way possible for you to have it both ways; at least not if you plan to go with Christ. Oil and water just don't mix.

Pause—Listen—Reflect

* * * * * * * * *

How Dare You?

How dare you? Have you lost your mind? You need to put a lid on it. No, I take that back. Cut it to shreds. Better yet, burn it. Grind it to ashes. Mix it in with the water and go ahead and drink it, all of it. Have a drink or take a bite:

> Exodus 32:19, 20—"When they came near the camp, Moses saw the calf and the dancing, and he burned with anger. He threw the stone tablets to the ground, smashing them at the foot of the mountain. (20) He took the calf they had made and burned it. Then he ground it into powder, threw it into the water, and forced the people to drink it" (NLT).

This may seem harsh, even bordering on being inhumane. But there comes a time when you are forced to throw down the gauntlet. This we do because our worship belongs to nothing or none other than the only one true and living God. There is simply no wiggle room; absolutely no exceptions here. This is set in stone; written in indelible ink. The one true God, YHWH is His name. So sacred is His name such that it is forbidden by some to ever address Him by His personal name. So yes, how dare you toy around with His worship? Have you lost it?

Pause—Listen—Reflect

* * * * * * * * *

Home

We live in a place we are reluctant to call home at times. We call to mind a place we once dubbed *home*, but we dare not return there. Now we look forward to a place we aspire to make our eternal home, somewhere beyond the wild blue yonder, sometime in the far distant future. Where is that? Have a drink or take a bite:

> Hebrews 11:8–10—"By faith Abraham, when he was called to go out into a place which he should after receive for an inheritance, obeyed; and he went out, not knowing whither he went. (9) By faith he sojourned in the land of promise, as in a strange country, dwelling in tabernacles with Isaac and Jacob, the heirs with him of the same promise: (10) For he looked for a city which hath foundations, whose builder and maker is God."

> Hebrews 13:14—"For here have we no continuing city, but we seek one to come."

> Revelation 21:10–12, 14, 16, 18–23, 25, 27—"And he carried me away in the spirit to a great and high mountain, and shewed me that great city, the holy Jerusalem, descending out of heaven from God, (11) having the glory of God: and her light was like unto a stone most precious, even like a jasper stone, clear as crystal; (12) and had a wall great

and high, and had twelve gates, and at the gates twelve angels... (14) And the wall of the city had twelve foundations, and in them the names of the twelve apostles of the Lamb... (16) And the city lieth foursquare, and the length is as large as the breadth: and he measured the city with the reed, twelve thousand furlongs. The length and the breadth and the height of it are equal... (18) And the building of the wall of it was of jasper: and the city was pure gold, like unto clear glass. (19) And the foundations of the wall of the city were garnished with all manner of precious stones. The first foundation was jasper; the second, sapphire; the third, a chalcedony; the fourth, an emerald; (20) the fifth, sardonyx; the sixth, sardius; the seventh, chrysolite; the eighth, beryl; the ninth, a topaz; the tenth, a chrysoprasus; the eleventh, a jacinth; the twelfth, an amethyst. (21) And the twelve gates were twelve pearls; every several gate was of one pearl: and the street of the city was pure gold, as it were transparent glass. (22) And I saw no temple therein: for the Lord God Almighty and the Lamb are the temple of it. (23) And the city had no need of the sun, neither of the moon, to shine in it: for the glory of God did lighten it, and the Lamb is the light thereof... (25) And the gates of it shall not be shut at all by day: for there shall be no night there... (27) And there shall in no wise enter into it any thing that defileth, neither whatsoever worketh abomination, or maketh a lie: but they which are written in the Lamb's book of life."

This is not coming from someone living on Fantasy Island. It is determinedly not a figment of one's imagination. Assuredly this is no wishful thinking, either. It is referring confidently to the believer's eternal residential home beyond the skies. Unquestionably. Undoubtedly.

Pause—Listen—Reflect

* * * * * * * * *

Mad Scientist

Someone a long time ago said of me, once I mount the pulpit and get started, I am off and running like a mad scientist. Another shared with me while working out that I made him tired just by watching me warming up. Well, that is my approach to most things I resolve to occupy myself with. I give it everything I have, putting my back into it. No holds barred. And I see absolutely nothing wrong with that. I am convinced that's how we all should approach life. Give it all you've got. We only have one shot at it. Have a drink or take a bite:

> 2 Samuel 6:14, 16—"And David danced before the Lord with all his might... (16) And as the ark of the Lord came into the city of David, Michal Saul's daughter looked through a window, and saw king David leaping and dancing before the Lord; and she despised him in her heart."

> Ecclesiastes 9:10—"Whatsoever thy hand findeth to do, do it with thy might; for there is no work, nor device, nor knowledge, nor wisdom, in the grave, whither thou goest."

> Luke 9:62—"And Jesus said unto him, No man, having put his hand to the plough, and looking back, is fit for the kingdom of God."

> Romans 12:11—"Not slothful in business; fervent in spirit; serving the Lord..."

> Colossians 3:23—"And whatsoever ye do, do it heartily, as to the Lord, and not unto men..."

I am persuaded, if you are going to commit to something, be all in. Forge ahead; no looking back. Well, OK, it's permissible to take a glance back every now and then, but only to see how far you've come. Then do an about-face and be right back on your merry way. Forward, not backward.

Pause—Listen—Reflect

* * * * * * * *

Closer

Come here, my friend. Come closer, a little closer. No worries, closer still. Yes, right there. That's good, thanks. Have a drink or take a bite:

> Isaiah 48:16, 17—"Come ye near unto me, hear ye this; I have not spoken in secret from the beginning; from the time that it was, there am I: And now the Lord God, and his Spirit, hath sent me. (17) Thus saith the Lord, thy Redeemer, the Holy One of Israel; I am the Lord thy God which teacheth thee to profit, which leadeth thee by the way that thou shouldest go."

> John 15:9–17—"As the Father hath loved me, so have I loved you: continue ye in my love. (10) If ye keep my commandments, ye shall abide in my love; even as I have kept my Father's commandments, and abide in his love. (11) These things

have I spoken unto you, that my joy might remain in you, and that your joy might be full. (12) This is my commandment, That ye love one another, as I have loved you. (13) Greater love hath no man than this, that a man lay down his life for his friends. (14) Ye are my friends, if ye do whatsoever I command you. (15) Henceforth I call you not servants; for the servant knoweth not what his lord doeth: but I have called you friends; for all things that I have heard of my Father I have made known unto you. (16) Ye have not chosen me, but I have chosen you, and ordained you, that ye should go and bring forth fruit, and that your fruit should remain: that whatsoever ye shall ask of the Father in my name, he may give it you. (17) These things I command you, that ye love one another."

Wow! This truly caught me off guard. Did you feel that? Anyone else feel what I felt? I was not expecting that. It is so overwhelming. *Grazie mille*, Lord. Thank You. We really needed that. Can we just remain right here for a little while longer?

Pause—Listen—Reflect

* * * * * * * * *

Stop

On your mark, get set, *stop!* Hold on. That's not what comes next. That's not how it is supposed to go. What's going on here? Have a drink or take a bite:

Acts 8:26–31, 35, 36, 38, 39—"And the angel of the Lord spake unto Philip, saying, Arise, and go toward the south unto the way that goeth down from Jerusalem unto Gaza, which is desert. (27) And he arose and went: and, behold, a man of Ethiopia, an eunuch of great authority under Candace queen of the Ethiopians, who had the charge of all her treasure, and had come to Jerusalem for to worship, (28) was returning, and sitting in his chariot read Esaias the prophet. (29) Then the Spirit said unto Philip, Go near, and join thyself to this chariot. (30) And Philip ran thither to him, and heard him read the prophet Esaias, and said, Understandest thou what thou readest? (31) And he said, How can I, except some man should guide me? And he desired Philip that he would come up and sit with him... (35) Then Philip opened his mouth, and began at the same scripture, and preached unto him Jesus. (36) And as they went on their way, they came unto a certain water: and the eunuch said, See, here is water; what doth hinder me to be baptized?... (38) And he commanded the chariot to stand still: and they went down both into the water, both Philip and the eunuch; and he baptized him. (39) And when they were come up out of the water, the Spirit of the Lord caught away Philip, that the eunuch saw him no more: and he went on his way rejoicing."

Acts 15:36–39—"And some days after Paul said unto Barnabas, Let us go again and visit our brethren in every city where we have preached the word of the Lord, and see how they do. (37) And Barnabas determined to take with them John, whose surname was Mark. (38) But Paul thought not good to take him with them, who departed from them from Pamphylia, and went not with them to the work. (39) And the contention was so sharp between them, that they departed asunder one from the other..."

Sometimes just as you are about to approach the finish line or rise to the pinnacle of life, right before the celebration begins, all the wheels fall off. Everything grinds to a screeching halt. Disappointing? You bet it is. Nonetheless, never let that get you down. Take heart in knowing that God always has greater plans. His plans are far better than what you had in mind.

Pause—Listen—Reflect

* * * * * * * *

Pray

Oh, how I long to be able to pray like that. It seems as though it comes so easily for you. Do you believe it's possible for me to pray as you do? Really? Is it? You've got to be kidding me. Well then, where do I begin? Have a drink or take a bite:

> Luke 11:1—"And it came to pass, that, as he was praying in a certain place, when he ceased, one of his disciples said unto him, Lord, teach us to pray, as John also taught his disciples."

> Matthew 6:5–13—"And when thou prayest, thou shalt not be as the hypocrites are: for they love to pray standing in the synagogues and in the corners of the streets, that they may be seen of men. Verily I say unto you, They have their reward. (6) But thou, when thou prayest, enter into thy closet, and when thou hast shut thy door, pray to thy Father which is in secret; and thy Father which seeth in secret shall reward thee openly. (7) But when ye pray, use not vain repetitions, as the heathen do: for they think that they shall be heard for their much speaking. (8) Be not ye therefore like unto them: for your Father knoweth what things ye have

need of, before ye ask him. (9) After this manner therefore pray ye: Our Father which art in heaven, Hallowed be thy name. (10) Thy kingdom come. Thy will be done in earth, as it is in heaven. (11) Give us this day our daily bread. (12) And forgive us our debts, as we forgive our debtors. (13) And lead us not into temptation, but deliver us from evil: For thine is the kingdom, and the power, and the glory, forever. Amen."

Mark 11:24, 25—"Therefore I say unto you, What things soever ye desire, when ye pray, believe that ye receive them, and ye shall have them. (25) And when ye stand praying, forgive, if ye have ought against any: that your Father also which is in heaven may forgive you your trespasses."

Thanks much, sir. It sure sounds simple enough, and straightforward too. This helps a whole lot. I'm ready now to give it a try. Let me see: "Our Father, who are in heaven, holy is Your name...Amen."

Pause—Listen—Reflect

* * * * * * * * *

Not So Fast

Resist the urge to pull the trigger so fast. Make sure you are certain it is all clear before you commence firing down range. Also, before you forget, properly calibrate your sight alignment. You are not ready until you have taken these critical safety measures. Have a drink or take a bite:

Ecclesiastes 5:2—"Don't shoot off your mouth, or speak before you think. Don't be too quick to

41

tell God what you think he wants to hear. God's in charge, not you—the less you speak, the better" (MSG).

Proverbs 10:19—"In the multitude of words there wanteth not sin: But he that refraineth his lips is wise."

Matthew 6:7, 8—"But when ye pray, use not vain repetitions, as the heathen do: for they think that they shall be heard for their much speaking. (8) Be not ye therefore like unto them: for your Father knoweth what things ye have need of, before ye ask him."

James 1:19—"Wherefore, my beloved brethren, let every man be swift to hear, slow to speak, slow to wrath..."

Not so fast. Pay attention to the OFF LIMITS signs. No rapid fire allowed. There are numerous restricted areas up ahead. Proceed with caution.

Pause—Listen—Reflect

* * * * * * * * *

Grand Slam

Who's up next? Who? Oh, no, not Him. Are you sure? Yes, Him! We might as well begin walking the bases right now, then. I see a home run coming. He is about to knock this one clear out of the park. All the bases are loaded too. Let's just call this a grand slam. Pack your bags, gents. Game over. It's time to go home. Have a drink or take a bite:

Deuteronomy 18:15, 18—"The Lord your God will raise up for you a Prophet like me from your midst, from your brethren. Him you shall hear... (18) I will raise up for them a Prophet like you from among their brethren, and will put My words in His mouth, and He shall speak to them all that I command Him" (NKJV).

Isaiah 11:1, 2, 10—"There shall come forth a Rod from the stem of Jesse, and a Branch shall grow out of his roots. (2) The Spirit of the Lord shall rest upon Him, the Spirit of wisdom and understanding, the Spirit of counsel and might, the Spirit of knowledge and of the fear of the Lord... (10) And in that day there shall be a Root of Jesse, who shall stand as a banner to the people; for the Gentiles shall seek Him, and His resting place shall be glorious" (NKJV).

Matthew 21:5, 7–9—"Tell the daughter of Zion, 'Behold, your King is coming to you, lowly, and sitting on a donkey, a colt, the foal of a donkey...' (7) They brought the donkey and the colt, laid their clothes on them, and set Him on them. (8) And a very great multitude spread their clothes on the road; others cut down branches from the trees and spread them on the road. (9) Then the multitudes who went before and those who followed cried out, saying: 'Hosanna to the Son of David' 'Blessed is He who comes in the name of the Lord!' Hosanna in the highest!" (NKJV).

John 1:19, 20, 23, 26, 27, 29, 30–36—"Now this is the testimony of John, when the Jews sent priests and Levites from Jerusalem to ask him, 'Who are you?' (20) He confessed, and did not deny, but confessed, 'I am not the Christ...' (23) He said: 'I am the voice of one crying in the wilderness: make straight the way of the Lord...' (26) John answered them, saying, 'I baptize with water, but there stands One among you whom you do not know. (27) It is He who, coming after me, is preferred before me, whose sandal strap I am not worthy to loose.'... (29) The next day John saw Jesus coming toward him, and said, 'Behold! The Lamb of God who takes away the sin of the world! (30) This is He of whom I said, "After me comes a Man who is preferred before me, for He was before me." (31) I did not know Him; but that He should be revealed to Israel, therefore I came baptizing with water.' (32) And John bore witness, saying, 'I saw the Spirit descending from heaven like a dove, and He remained upon Him. (33) I did not know Him, but He who sent me to baptize with water said to me, "Upon whom you see the Spirit descending, and remaining on Him, this is He who baptizes with the Holy Spirit." (34) And I have seen and testified that this is the Son of God.' (35) Again, the next day, John stood with two of his disciples. (36) And looking at Jesus as He walked, he said, 'Behold the Lamb of God!'" (NKJV).

Acts 13:23—"From this man's seed, according to the promise, God raised up for Israel a Savior—Jesus" (NKJV).

Revelation 5:2–10—"Then I saw a strong angel proclaiming with a loud voice, 'Who is worthy to open the scroll and to loose its seals?' (3) And no one in heaven or on the earth or under the earth was able to open the scroll, or to look at it. (4) So I wept much, because no one was found worthy to open and read the scroll, or to look at it. (5) But one of the elders said to me, 'Do not weep. Behold, the Lion of the tribe of Judah, the Root of David, has prevailed to open the scroll and to loose its seven seals.' (6) And I looked, and behold, in the midst of the throne and of the four living creatures, and in the midst of the elders, stood a Lamb as though it had been slain... (7) Then He came and took the scroll out of the right hand of Him who sat on the throne. (8) Now when He had taken the scroll, the four living creatures and the twenty-four elders fell down before the Lamb, each having a harp, and golden bowls full of incense... (9) And they sang a new song, saying: 'You are worthy to take the scroll, and to open its seals; for You were slain, and have redeemed us to God by Your blood out of every tribe and tongue and people and nation, (10) And have made us kings and priests to our God...'" (NKJV).

No, there was none before Him. There is none besides Him. And surely there will never be another like unto Him. He is indeed the heavy hitter par excellence. There are strictly no comparisons. It's a grand slam. All that's left is to walk the bases. Game over. Let's go home.

Pause—Listen—Reflect

* * * * * * * * *

Bumper Stickers

I keep running into these bumper stickers that read, JESUS IS THE ANSWER. I cannot help but wonder: *what's the question?* Then I was enlightened. It doesn't matter what the question is. Jesus "Is!" no matter the question. Have a drink or take a bite:

Ephesians 1:20–23—"When he raised him from the dead, and set him at his own right hand in the heavenly places, (21) Far above all principality, and power, and might, and dominion, and every name that is named, not only in this world, but also in that which is to come: (22) And hath put all things under his feet, and gave him to be the head over all things to the church, (23) which is his body, the fulness of him that filleth all in all."

Revelation 22:13—"I'm A to Z, the First and the Final, the Beginning and the Conclusion!" (MSG).

This is good stuff right here. Fitting of a king, the King of kings. He did mention that He and the Father are one (Jn. 10:30). Therefore, that also makes Him the "I am that I am" (Exod. 3:14).

Pause—Listen—Reflect

* * * * * * * *

Poisoned Pill

Do not fall for his age-old scheme. He already has a dungeon full of credulous ones who didn't catch on soon enough to escape his vices. If not from me, take it from them. You do not want to be his next victim. It's a poisoned pill. Heed this advice. Have a drink or take a bite:

Genesis 3:4–7—"And the serpent said unto the woman, Ye shall not surely die: (5) For God doth know that in the day ye eat thereof, then your eyes shall be opened, and ye shall be as gods, knowing good and evil. (6) And when the woman saw that the tree was good for food, and that it was pleasant to the eyes, and a tree to be desired to make one wise, she took of the fruit thereof, and did eat, and gave also unto her husband with her; and he did eat. (7) And the eyes of them both were opened, and they knew that they were naked; and they sewed fig leaves together, and made themselves aprons."

2 Corinthians 11:3, 4—"But I fear, lest by any means, as the serpent beguiled Eve through his subtilty, so your minds should be corrupted from the simplicity that is in Christ. (4) For if he that cometh preacheth another Jesus, whom we have not preached, or if ye receive another spirit, which ye have not received, or another gospel, which ye have not accepted, ye might well bear with him."

1 Thessalonians 3:5—"For this cause, when I could no longer forbear, I sent to know your faith, lest by some means the tempter have tempted you, and our labour be in vain."

Revelation 12:9—"And the great dragon was cast out, that old serpent, called the Devil, and Satan, which deceiveth the whole world: he was cast out into the earth, and his angels were cast out with him."

Look from whence we've fallen. That is how we arrived where we are now. Oh my, what a tangled web we weaved. Do you see where all that has gotten us? Don't be the next one to swallow another poisoned pill of his. Surely you have learned better by now. There's a wealth of truth in Benjamin Franklin's advice: "An ounce of prevention is worth a pound of cure."

Pause—Listen—Reflect

* * * * * * * * *

Expand

In order to reach your full capability to accommodate the greater blessing that's on its way, you must enlarge your territory. Where you are now works marvelously to contain your present blessings, but it's totally inadequate for what is on its way. Have a drink or take a bite:

> 1 Chronicles 4:10—"Oh, that You would bless me and expand my territory! Please be with me in all that I do, and keep me from all trouble and pain!" And God granted him his request" (NLT).

> Luke 5:36–38—"And he spake also a parable unto them; No man putteth a piece of a new garment upon an old; if otherwise, then both the new maketh a rent, and the piece that was taken out of the new agreeth not with the old. (37) And no man putteth new wine into old bottles; else the new wine will burst the bottles, and be spilled, and the bottles shall perish. (38) But new wine must be put into new bottles; and both are preserved."

What's coming is greater than what's here. It cannot be contained in your current territory. You must tear down walls, chop down hedges, and dig up roots. Push out. Invest all you have. Prepare to expand.

Pause—Listen—Reflect

* * * * * * * * *

Why

I've been wondering: *why do all these things seem to be working against me?* Then it dawned on me. Have a drink or take a bite:

48

> Psalm 119:71—"My suffering was good for me, for
> it taught me to pay attention to your decrees" (NLT).

Now I'm rejoicing. Hallelujah! What I once thought was working against me, I now know it was working for my good. I'm no longer wondering *Why?* Thank you, Jesus.

Pause—Listen—Reflect

* * * * * * * *

The Great Escape

The one that got away, the big fish, that's the one we will never get enough of talking about. We are forever elated whenever the underdog suddenly surfaces as the hero or heroine. And the plot thickens. Have a drink or take a bite:

> Genesis 27:41–45—"So Esau hated Jacob because
> of the blessing with which his father blessed him,
> and Esau said in his heart, 'The days of mourning
> for my father are at hand; then I will kill my brother
> Jacob.' (42) And the words of Esau her older son
> were told to Rebekah. So she sent and called Jacob
> her younger son, and said to him, 'Surely your
> brother Esau comforts himself concerning you by
> intending to kill you. (43) Now therefore, my son,
> obey my voice: arise, flee to my brother Laban in
> Haran. (44) And stay with him a few days, until your
> brother's fury turns away, (45) until your brother's
> anger turns away from you, and he forgets what you
> have done to him; then I will send and bring you
> from there. Why should I be bereaved also of you
> both in one day?'" (NKJV).

Genesis 28:1, 2, 10—"Then Isaac called Jacob and blessed him... (2) Arise, go to Padan Aram, to the house of Bethuel your mother's father... (5) So Isaac sent Jacob away, and he went to Padan Aram... (10) Now Jacob went out from Beersheba and went toward Haran" (NKJV).

1 Kings 19:1–3—"And Ahab told Jezebel all that Elijah had done, also how he had executed all the prophets with the sword. (2) Then Jezebel sent a messenger to Elijah, saying, 'So let the gods do to me, and more also, if I do not make your life as the life of one of them by tomorrow about this time.' (3) And when he saw that, he arose and ran for his life, and went to Beersheba..." (NKJV).

Judges 15:12–14—"'We have come down to arrest you, that we may deliver you into the hand of the Philistines.' Then Samson said to them, 'Swear to me that you will not kill me yourselves.' (13) So they spoke to him, saying, 'No, but we will tie you securely and deliver you into their hand; but we will surely not kill you.' And they bound him with two new ropes and brought him up from the rock. (14) When he came to Lehi, the Philistines came shouting against him. Then the Spirit of the Lord came mightily upon him; and the ropes that were on his arms became like flax that is burned with fire, and his bonds broke loose from his hands" (NKJV).

1 Samuel 18:8–11—"Then Saul was very angry, and the saying displeased him; and he said, 'They have ascribed to David ten thousands, and to me they have ascribed only thousands. Now what more can he have but the kingdom?' (9) So Saul eyed David from that day forward. (10) And it happened on the next day that the distressing spirit from God came upon

Saul, and he prophesied inside the house. So David played music with his hand, as at other times; but there was a spear in Saul's hand. (11) And Saul cast the spear, for he said, 'I will pin David to the wall!' But David escaped his presence twice" (NKJV).

1 Samuel 19:9–12—"Now the distressing spirit from the Lord came upon Saul as he sat in his house with his spear in his hand. And David was playing music with his hand. (10) Then Saul sought to pin David to the wall with the spear, but he slipped away from Saul's presence; and he drove the spear into the wall. So David fled and escaped that night. (11) Saul also sent messengers to David's house to watch him and to kill him in the morning. And Michal, David's wife, told him, saying, 'If you do not save your life tonight, tomorrow you will be killed.' (12) So Michal let David down through a window. And he went and fled and escaped" (NKJV).

1 Samuel 21:11–15—"And the servants of Achish said to him, 'Is this not David the king of the land? Did they not sing of him to one another in dances, saying: "Saul has slain his thousands, and David his ten thousands'?" (12) Now David took these words to heart, and was very much afraid of Achish the king of Gath. (13) So he changed his behavior before them, pretended madness in their hands, scratched on the doors of the gate, and let his saliva fall down on his beard. (14) Then Achish said to his servants, 'Look, you see the man is insane. Why have you brought him to me? (15) Have I need of madmen, that you have brought this fellow to play the madman in my presence? Shall this fellow come into my house?'" (NKJV).

1 Samuel 22:1—"David therefore departed from there and escaped to the cave of Adullam" (NKJV).

Acts 5:17–23, 25—"Then the high priest rose up, and all those who were with him (which is the sect of the Sadducees), and they were filled with indignation, (18) and laid their hands on the apostles and put them in the common prison. (19) But at night an angel of the Lord opened the prison doors and brought them out, and said, (20) 'Go, stand in the temple and speak to the people all the words of this life.' (21) And when they heard that, they entered the temple early in the morning and taught. But the high priest and those with him came and called the council together, with all the elders of the children of Israel, and sent to the prison to have them brought. (22) But when the officers came and did not find them in the prison, they returned and reported, (23) saying, 'Indeed we found the prison shut securely, and the guards standing outside before the doors; but when we opened them, we found no one inside!'... (25) So one came and told them, saying, 'Look, the men whom you put in prison are standing in the temple and teaching the people!'" (NKJV).

Acts 16:25, 26—"But at midnight Paul and Silas were praying and singing hymns to God, and the prisoners were listening to them. (26) Suddenly there was a great earthquake, so that the foundations of the prison were shaken; and immediately all the doors were opened and everyone's chains were loosed" (NKJV).

Matthew 28:1–6—"Now after the Sabbath, as the first day of the week began to dawn, Mary Magdalene and the other Mary came to see the tomb. (2) And behold, there was a great earthquake; for an angel of the Lord descended from heaven, and came and rolled back the stone from the door, and sat on it. (3) His countenance was like lightning, and his clothing as white as snow. (4) And the guards shook for fear of him, and became like dead men. (5) But the angel answered and said to the women, 'Do not be afraid, for I know that you seek Jesus who was crucified. (6) He is not here; for He is risen, as He said. Come, see the place where the Lord lay'" (NKJV).

Luke 24:1–7—"Now on the first day of the week, very early in the morning, they, and certain other women with them, came to the tomb bringing the spices which they had prepared. (2) But they found the stone rolled away from the tomb. (3) Then they went in and did not find the body of the Lord Jesus. (4) And it happened, as they were greatly perplexed about this, that behold, two men stood by them in shining garments. (5) Then, as they were afraid and bowed their faces to the earth, they said to them, 'Why do you seek the living among the dead? (6) He is not here, but is risen! Remember how He spoke to you when He was still in Galilee, (7) saying, "The Son of Man must be delivered into the hands of sinful men, and be crucified, and the third day rise again"'" (NKJV).

Since Satan couldn't seal the deal, having you right within his reach, what makes him believe he can snatch you from the Master's grasp now? The villain may be assigned very significant roles in the overall plot, but he's not the one who determines the story's ending. With your Lord's help, you, too, have managed to pull off the great escape. There's no seizing you now.

Pause—Listen—Reflect

* * * * * * * * *

Heads-Up

Now that resembles a screaming line drive. Or is it more like a fastball? Either way, heads up. Coming right atcha. You best be nimble and be quick. Act fast. Have a drink or take a bite:

> John 6:67, 68—"Then said Jesus unto the twelve, Will ye also go away? (68) Then Simon Peter answered him, Lord, to whom shall we go? thou hast the words of eternal life."

> Matthew 16:15, 16—"He saith unto them, But whom say ye that I am? (16) And Simon Peter answered and said, Thou art the Christ, the Son of the living God."

I would say that was a bullet. A true screaming line drive, for sure. Sometimes they show up on short notice. At other times, they give no notice at all. They can be easily fumbled. Are you a catcher or fumbler?

Pause—Listen—Reflect

* * * * * * * * *

Deafening Silence

The silence is deafening in here. Is anyone going to say something? It is so quiet I hear pins striking the dust. Somebody, anybody, please speak up. Have a drink or take a bite:

> Mark 3:4—"And he saith unto them, Is it lawful to do good on the sabbath days, or to do evil? to save life, or to kill? But they held their peace."

> Mark 9:33, 34—"What was it that ye disputed among yourselves by the way? (34) But they held their peace: for by the way they had disputed among themselves, who should be the greatest."

> Luke 20:26—"And they could not take hold of his words before the people: and they marvelled at his answer, and held their peace."

> John 8:7–9—"So when they continued asking him, he lifted up himself, and said unto them, He that is without sin among you, let him first cast a stone at her. (8) And again he stooped down, and wrote on the ground. (9) And they which heard it, being convicted by their own conscience, went out one by one, beginning at the eldest, even unto the last: and Jesus was left alone, and the woman standing in the midst."

That is it right there. That's the appropriate note to strike. Whenever you are the guilty party, if you are not repentant, it's in your best interest to keep silent. It is your foremost posture to assume if you choose to remain defiant. No need to hem yourself in any further. You will never find your way out. Sometimes silence is golden.

Pause—Listen—Reflect

* * * * * * * * *

Strike a Balance

Go fast, and be accused of leaving some behind. Go slow, and you're accused of lagging behind. Shouted down if you dare speed things up, yelled at for slowing it down. What can a brother or sister do? Are you at a loss for how to handle it? Have a drink or take a bite:

Romans 14:1—"Him that is weak in the faith receive ye, but not to doubtful disputations."

Romans 15:1, 2—"We then that are strong ought to bear the infirmities of the weak, and not to please ourselves. (2) Let every one of us please his neighbour for his good to edification."

1 Corinthians 9:19–23—"For though I be free from all men, yet have I made myself servant unto all, that I might gain the more. (20) And unto the Jews I became as a Jew, that I might gain the Jews; to them that are under the law, as under the law, that I might gain them that are under the law; (21) To them that are without law, as without law, (being not without law to God, but under the law to Christ,) that I might gain them that are without law. (22) To the weak became I as weak, that I might gain the weak: I am made all things to all men, that I might by all means save some. (23) And this I do for the gospel's sake..."

1 Corinthians 10:31–33—"Whether therefore ye eat, or drink, or whatsoever ye do, do all to the glory of God. (32) Give none offence, neither to the Jews, nor to the Gentiles, nor to the church of God: (33) Even as I please all men in all things, not seeking mine own profit, but the profit of many, that they may be saved."

1 Corinthians 11:1—"Be ye followers of me, even as I also am of Christ."

Make the necessary adjustments. Find a way to strike a balance. In this unique instance, teeter tottering is not so bad after all. It's a delicate balancing act.

Pause—Listen—Reflect

* * * * * * * * *

Slip Showing

That surely is a beautiful outfit you are wearing today. There is only one problem, though: your slip is showing. After all that valuable time you spent getting yourself together, that definitely ruins everything. Have a drink or take a bite:

> Ezekiel 8:5–10, 12, 13, 15—"Then the Lord said to me, 'Son of man, look toward the north.' So I looked, and there to the north, beside the entrance to the gate near the altar, stood the idol that had made the Lord so jealous. (6) 'Son of man,' he said, 'do you see what they are doing? Do you see the detestable sins the people of Israel are committing to drive me from my Temple? But come, and you will see even more detestable sins than these!' (7) Then he brought me to the door of the Temple courtyard, where I could see a hole in the wall. (8) He said to me, 'Now, son of man, dig into the wall.' So I dug into the wall and found a hidden doorway. (9) 'Go in,' he said, 'and see the wicked and detestable sins they are committing in there!' (10) So I went in and saw the walls covered with engravings of all kinds of crawling animals and detestable creatures. I also saw the various idols worshiped by the people of Israel... (12) Then the Lord said to me, 'Son of man, have you seen what the leaders of Israel are doing with

their idols in dark rooms? They are saying, "The Lord doesn't see us; he has deserted our land!'" (13) Then the Lord added, 'Come, and I will show you even more detestable sins than these!'... (15) 'Have you seen this?' he asked. 'But I will show you even more detestable sins than these!'" (NLT).

Job 34:21, 22—"For his eyes are upon the ways of man, and he seeth all his goings. (22) There is no darkness, nor shadow of death, where the workers of iniquity may hide themselves."

Proverbs 15:3—"The eyes of the Lord are in every place, beholding the evil and the good."

Jeremiah 16:17—"For mine eyes are upon all their ways: they are not hid from my face, neither is their iniquity hid from mine eyes."

Hebrews 4:13—"Neither is there any creature that is not manifest in his sight: but all things are naked and opened unto the eyes of him with whom we have to do."

Do not be deceived. A word of caution to the wise: everything happening in private, all behind closed doors, know that watchful eyes are looking on. The all-seeing eye of God sees everything. He misses nothing.

Pause—Listen—Reflect

* * * * * * * *

Give Back

It was all Mine long before it became yours. Give it back and it will still remain yours. You will find, when you do, you gain even more. Lots more. Who would have thought something as this could be possible? Have a drink or take a bite:

> 2 Chronicles 31:5, 6, 9, 10—"And as soon as the commandment came abroad, the children of Israel brought in abundance the firstfruits of corn, wine, and oil, and honey, and of all the increase of the field; and the tithe of all things brought they in abundantly. (6) ...they also brought in the tithe of oxen and sheep, and the tithe of holy things which were consecrated unto the Lord their God, and laid them by heaps... (9) Then Hezekiah questioned with the priests and the Levites concerning the heaps. (10) And Azariah the chief priest of the house of Zadok answered him, and said, Since the people began to bring the offerings into the house of the Lord, we have had enough to eat, and have left plenty: for the Lord hath blessed his people; and that which is left is this great store."

> Proverbs 3:9,10—"Honour the Lord with thy substance, and with the firstfruits of all thine increase: (10) So shall thy barns be filled with plenty, and thy presses shall burst out with new wine."

> Malachi 3:10–12—"Bring ye all the tithes into the storehouse, that there may be meat in mine house, and prove me now herewith, saith the Lord of hosts, if I will not open you the windows of heaven, and pour you out a blessing, that there shall not be room enough to receive it. (11) And I will rebuke the devourer for your sakes, and he shall not destroy the fruits of your ground; neither

shall your vine cast her fruit before the time in the field, saith the Lord of hosts. (12) And all nations shall call you blessed: For ye shall be a delightsome land, saith the Lord of hosts."

Your tithes and offerings, when you give it back, you gain even more. Lots more. Does this sound backward or even upside down to you? Maybe even foolish? I dare you, double-dog dare you. Do as it says and watch God work.

Pause—Listen—Reflect

* * * * * * * * *

There's Room

Can anyone else fit in there? It doesn't look like it to me. And imagine—there's still a line a mile long out here. There has to be another way. Let's see if we can find one. Have a drink or take a bite:

> Isaiah 5:14—"Therefore hell hath enlarged herself, and opened her mouth without measure: And their glory, and their multitude, and their pomp, and he that rejoiceth, shall descend into it."

> Matthew 7:13, 14—"Enter ye in at the strait gate: for wide is the gate, and broad is the way, that leadeth to destruction, and many there be which go in thereat: (14) Because strait is the gate, and narrow is the way, which leadeth unto life, and few there be that find it."

It is fiery hot and tormenting in there. And that is where the line you are standing leads. Are you sure you still want to wait in that long, everlasting line? Look, there is plenty of room over here.

There is no line either. Why don't you come on over? You'll be much better off, if you do.

Pause—Listen—Reflect

* * * * * * * * *

Overconfidence

I've got this down to a science, done it a thousand times with my eyes closed. I can do it in my sleep, all by myself. I need nobody's help. I got this! No sweat! Is that so? Really? Have a drink or take a bite:

> Judges 16:20, 21—"And she said, The Philistines be upon thee, Samson. And he awoke out of his sleep, and said, I will go out as at other times before, and shake myself. And he wist not that the Lord was departed from him. (21) But the Philistines took him, and put out his eyes, and brought him down to Gaza, and bound him with fetters of brass; and he did grind in the prison house."

> Isaiah 14:12–15—"How art thou fallen from heaven, O Lucifer, son of the morning! How art thou cut down to the ground, which didst weaken the nations! (13) For thou hast said in thine heart, I will ascend into heaven, I will exalt my throne above the stars of God: I will sit also upon the mount of the congregation, in the sides of the north: (14) I will ascend above the heights of the clouds; I will be like the most High. (15) Yet thou shalt be brought down to hell, to the sides of the pit."

Romans 11:20, 21—"Be not highminded, but fear: (21) For if God spared not the natural branches, take heed lest he also spare not thee."

Romans 12:3—"For I say, through the grace given unto me, to every man that is among you, not to think of himself more highly than he ought to think; but to think soberly, according as God hath dealt to every man the measure of faith."

1 Corinthians 10:12—"Wherefore let him that thinketh he standeth take heed lest he fall."

It's perfectly fine to remain confident. Yes, but keep it toned down. It is better to under-promise and over-deliver than to overpromise but underperform. Take a moment. Consider Lucifer. Consider the plight of Samson. Overconfidence can be your Achilles' heel.

Pause—Listen—Reflect

* * * * * * * *

Emergencies

We are knee deep in the midst of a five-alarm fire. Multiple, simultaneous 911 calls are coming in. The house is on fire. I have never seen anything the likes of this before. This is purely unbelievable. And you are doing what? You can't be serious. Nobody has got time for that right now, man. Are you kidding me? Have a drink or take a bite:

Jonah 1:4–6—"But the Lord sent out a great wind into the sea, and there was a mighty tempest in the sea, so that the ship was like to be broken. (5) Then the mariners were afraid, and cried every man unto his god, and cast forth the wares that were in the ship into the sea, to lighten it of them. But Jonah was gone down into the sides of the ship; and he lay, and was fast asleep. (6) So the shipmaster came to him, and said unto him, What meanest thou, O sleeper? arise, call upon thy God..."

Mark 4:37–40—"And there arose a great storm of wind, and the waves beat into the ship, so that it was now full. (38) And he was in the hinder part of the ship, asleep on a pillow: and they awake him, and say unto him, Master, carest thou not that we perish? (39) And he arose, and rebuked the wind, and said unto the sea, Peace, be still. And the wind ceased, and there was a great calm. (40) And he said unto them, Why are ye so fearful? how is it that ye have no faith?"

Acts 27:21, 22, 25, 30, 31, 34, 42–44—"But after long abstinence Paul stood forth in the midst of them, and said, Sirs, ye should have hearkened unto me, and not have loosed from Crete, and to have gained this harm and loss. (22) And now I exhort you to be of good cheer: for there shall be no loss of any man's life among you, but of the ship... (25) Wherefore, sirs, be of good cheer: for I believe God, that it shall be even as it was told me... (30) And as the shipmen were about to flee out of the ship, when they had let down the boat into the sea, under colour as though they would have cast anchors out of the foreship, (31) Paul said to the centurion and to the soldiers, Except these abide in the ship, ye cannot be saved... (34) Wherefore I pray you to take some meat: for this is for your health: for there shall not an hair fall from the head of any of you... (42) And the soldiers' counsel was to kill the prisoners, lest any of them should swim out, and escape. (43) But the centurion, willing to

save Paul, kept them from their purpose; and commanded that they which could swim should cast
themselves first into the sea, and get to land: (44)
And the rest, some on boards, and some on broken
pieces of the ship. And so it came to pass, that they
escaped all safe to land."

And so, everybody, please calm down. Not one single soul will
perish today. No, not on His watch. Regardless of how much water
your vessel takes on, remain calm. Things are going to work out
as promised. Just you wait and see.

Pause—Listen—Reflect

* * * * * * * *

Slow Down

Slow it down. Why are you in such a hurry? What's the rush?
Where are you heading so fast, anyway? Have a drink or take a bite:

James 1:19—"Wherefore, my beloved brethren, let
every man be swift to hear, slow to speak, slow
to wrath..."

Proverbs 14:17—"He that is soon angry dealeth
foolishly: And a man of wicked devices is hated."

Proverbs 16:32—"He that is slow to anger is better
than the mighty; and he that ruleth his spirit than
he that taketh a city."

Proverbs 19:11—"The discretion of a man defer-
reth his anger; and it is his glory to pass over a
transgression."

> Ecclesiastes 7:9—"Be not hasty in thy spirit to be angry: for anger resteth in the bosom of fools."

Do not be in such a hurry. Take your time. Slow your roll. Gather it up and pull yourself together.

Pause—Listen—Reflect

* * * * * * * * *

Honestly

Honestly speaking, things aren't looking good. They aren't sounding good, either; not at all. I really don't know how else to say it. The forecast looks extremely bleak. It is going to take a herculean effort to get through what's ahead.

This is the overwhelming feeling I'm left with after listening to the evening news on any given day. With all that is occurring around us, I have concluded it is going to take a herculean effort indeed. But hold on. This is not my final assessment. Don't give up hope quite yet. Just the right panacea for all these ills is now in sight. Have a drink or take a bite:

> Isaiah 6:8—"Also I heard the voice of the Lord, saying, Whom shall I send, and who will go for us? Then said I, Here am I; send me."

> Isaiah 9:6, 7—"For unto us a child is born, unto us a son is given: And the government shall be upon his shoulder: And his name shall be called Wonderful, Counselor, the mighty God, the everlasting Father, the Prince of Peace. (7) Of the increase of his government and peace there shall be no end, upon the throne of David, and upon his kingdom, to order it, and to establish it with judgment and with justice

from henceforth even forever. The zeal of the Lord
of hosts will perform this."

Matthew 28:18—"And Jesus came and spake unto
them, saying, All power is given unto me in heaven
and in earth."

Luke 2:11—"For unto you is born this day in the
city of David a Saviour, which is Christ the Lord."

Hebrews 10:5–7, 9—"Wherefore when he cometh
into the world, he saith, Sacrifice and offering thou
wouldest not, but a body hast thou prepared me: (6)
In burnt offerings and sacrifices for sin thou hast
had no pleasure. (7) Then said I, Lo, I come (in the
volume of the book it is written of me,) to do thy
will, O God... (9) Then said he, Lo, I come to do
thy will, O God. He taketh away the first, that he
may establish the second."

No worries, it's a cakewalk. Jesus saves the day. Every day. God
has got this wrapped up nicely. Not only that, He's got you too.
Only have faith in God. Full stop! Nothing further, just have
faith in God.

Pause—Listen—Reflect

* * * * * * * *

Backward and Forward

Forward facing yet backward moving — how do you ever expect
to reach your destination going backward? It will never happen.
Have a drink or take a bite:

Genesis 19:15–17, 22, 26—"And when the morning arose, then the angels hastened Lot, saying, Arise, take thy wife, and thy two daughters, which are here; lest thou be consumed in the iniquity of the city. (16) And while he lingered, the men laid hold upon his hand, and upon the hand of his wife, and upon the hand of his two daughters; the Lord being merciful unto him: and they brought him forth, and set him without the city. (17) And it came to pass, when they had brought them forth abroad, that he said, Escape for thy life; look not behind thee, neither stay thou in all the plain; escape to the mountain, lest thou be consumed... (22) Haste thee, escape thither; for I cannot do any thing till thou be come thither... (26) But his wife looked back from behind him, and she became a pillar of salt."

Proverbs 26:11—"As a dog returneth to his vomit, so a fool returneth to his folly."

Luke 9:62—"And Jesus said unto him, No man, having put his hand to the plough, and looking back, is fit for the kingdom of God."

Luke 17:31, 32—"In that day, he which shall be upon the housetop, and his stuff in the house, let him not come down to take it away: and he that is in the field, let him likewise not return back. (32) Remember Lot's wife."

2 Peter 2:22—"But it is happened unto them according to the true proverb, The dog is turned to his own vomit again; and the sow that was washed to her wallowing in the mire."

Never forget but evermore remember Lot's wife. Don't ever forget. A-ten-hut! Forward march!

Pause—Listen—Reflect

* * * * * * * * *

All for One

We are one team; all for one and one for all. Full stop! End of discussion; have a drink or take a bite:

> Joshua 22:20—"Did not Achan the son of Zerah commit a trespass in the accursed thing, and wrath fell on all the congregation of Israel? and that man perished not alone in his iniquity."

> Romans 5:12, 15, 17–19—"Wherefore, as by one man sin entered into the world, and death by sin; and so death passed upon all men, for that all have sinned... (15) For if through the offence of one many be dead, much more the grace of God, and the gift by grace, which is by one man, Jesus Christ, hath abounded unto many... (17) For if by one man's offence death reigned by one; much more they which receive abundance of grace and of the gift of righteousness shall reign in life by one, Jesus Christ.) (18) Therefore as by the offence of one judgment came upon all men to condemnation; even so by the righteousness of one the free gift came upon all men unto justification of life. (19) For as by one man's disobedience many were made sinners, so by the obedience of one shall many be made righteous."

Whenever you win, I win. By the same token, whenever you lose, I lose. It's either a win-win or lose-lose situation. You affect me as I affect you. Each one affects the other. Nothing happens in a vacuum. I humbly suggest that you seriously consider this principle before you take action the next time around.

Pause—Listen—Reflect

* * * * * * * * *

Doesn't Seem Fair

It just doesn't seem fair to me, not at all. Working my fingers to the bone; after all I've done—doing my utmost best to remain on the straight and narrow, dotting my *i's* and crossing my *t's*—you mean to tell me that I am still no better off than the next man? Lord, why me? Have a drink or take a bite:

> 1 Samuel 2:6–8—"The Lord kills and makes alive; He brings down to the grave and brings up. (7) The Lord makes poor and makes rich; He brings low and lifts up. (8) He raises the poor from the dust and lifts the beggar from the ash heap, to set them among princes and make them inherit the throne of glory" (NKJV).

> Job 1:21—"Naked I came from my mother's womb, and naked shall I return there. The Lord gave, and the Lord has taken away" (NKJV).

> Job 34:9–12—"For he has said, 'It profits a man nothing that he should delight in God.' (10) 'Therefore listen to me, you men of understanding: Far be it from God to do wickedness, and from the Almighty to commit iniquity. (11) For He repays man according to his work, and makes man to find

a reward according to his way. (12) Surely God will never do wickedly, nor will the Almighty pervert justice'" (NKJV).

Job 35:2, 3—"Do you think this is right? Do you say, 'My righteousness is more than God's'? (3) For you say, 'What advantage will it be to you? What profit shall I have, more than if I had sinned?'" (NKJV).

Psalm 27:12—"I would have lost heart, unless I had believed that I would see the goodness of the Lord in the land of the living" (NKJV).

Psalm 73:13, 14, 16, 17—"Surely I have cleansed my heart in vain, and washed my hands in innocence. (14) For all day long I have been plagued, and chastened every morning... (16) When I thought how to understand this, it was too painful for me—(17) until I went into the sanctuary of God; then I understood their end" (NKJV).

Isaiah 58:2—"'Why have we fasted,' they say, 'and You have not seen? Why have we afflicted our souls, and You take no notice?'" (NKJV).

Jeremiah 12:1, 2—"Yet let me talk with You about Your judgments. Why does the way of the wicked prosper? Why are those happy who deal so treacherously? (2) You have planted them, yes, they have taken root; they grow, yes, they bear fruit" (NKJV).

Ezekiel 18:25—"Yet you say, 'The way of the Lord is not fair.' Hear now, O house of Israel, is it not My way which is fair, and your ways which are not fair?" (NKJV).

Malachi 3:14, 15—"You have said, 'It is useless to serve God; what profit is it that we have kept His ordinance, and that we have walked as mourners before the Lord of hosts? (15) So now we call the proud blessed, for those who do wickedness are raised up; they even tempt God and go free'" (NKJV).

Matthew 5:45—"For He makes His sun rise on the evil and on the good, and sends rain on the just and on the unjust" (NKJV).

Philippians 4:11–13—"For I have learned in whatever state I am, to be content: (12) I know how to be abased, and I know how to abound. Everywhere and in all things I have learned both to be full and to be hungry, both to abound and to suffer need. (13) I can do all things through Christ who strengthens me" (NKJV).

1 Timothy 6:6, 7—"Now godliness with contentment is great gain. (7) For we brought nothing into this world, and it is certain we can carry nothing out" (NKJV).

Hebrews 13:5—"Let your conduct be without covetousness; be content with such things as you have. For He Himself has said, 'I will never leave you nor forsake you'" (NKJV).

All righteous, all faithful, sovereign God, we leave it all in Your capable hands. We are confident that You will work things out for our good. We trust Your handiwork, no matter what, even when it doesn't seem fair.

Pause—Listen—Reflect

* * * * * * * * *

Bald-Faced Liar

He is a bald-faced liar, a thief, and a deceiver too. Never believe a word he says. The closest he has ever been to truth is half-truths. But that still leaves him a bald-faced liar. Have a drink or take a bite:

> Luke 10:18—"And he said unto them, I beheld Satan as lightning fall from heaven."

> John 8:44—"Ye are of your father the devil, and the lusts of your father ye will do. He was a murderer from the beginning, and abode not in the truth, because there is no truth in him. When he speaketh a lie, he speaketh of his own: for he is a liar, and the father of it."

> John 10:10—"The thief cometh not, but for to steal, and to kill, and to destroy: I am come that they might have life, and that they might have it more abundantly."

> Revelation 20:3, 8, 10—"And cast him into the bottomless pit, and shut him up, and set a seal upon him, that he should deceive the nations no more, till the thousand years should be fulfilled: and after that he must be loosed a little season... (8) And shall go out to deceive the nations which are in the four quarters of the earth... (10) And the devil that

deceived them was cast into the lake of fire and brimstone, where the beast and the false prophet are, and shall be tormented day and night for ever and ever."

He simply cannot help himself. It's in his DNA. That is all he knows to do: lie and deceive. That is exactly what he is: a bald-faced liar. And let's not forget that he is also a thief, murderer, and troublemaker, too. He is destined to meet his reckoning. The wrath of God is reserved just for him.

Pause—Listen—Reflect

* * * * * * * *

Station Identification

Three, two, one, cut! Let's take five for station identification. Have a drink or take a bite:

> Numbers 24:17—"I shall see him, but not now: I shall behold him, but not nigh: There shall come a Star out of Jacob, and a Sceptre shall rise out of Israel..."

> Jeremiah 23:5, 6—"Behold, the days come, saith the Lord, that I will raise unto David a righteous Branch, and a King shall reign and prosper, and shall execute judgment and justice in the earth. (6) In his days Judah shall be saved, and Israel shall dwell safely: and this is his name whereby he shall be called, THE LORD OUR RIGHTEOUSNESS."

> Luke 1:78—"Through the tender mercy of our God; whereby the dayspring from on high hath visited us..."

1 Timothy 1:17—"Now unto the King eternal, immortal, invisible, the only wise God, be honour and glory for ever and ever. Amen."

1 Timothy 6:15, 16—"Which in his times he shall shew, who is the blessed and only Potentate, the King of kings, and Lord of lords; (16) who only hath immortality, dwelling in the light which no man can approach unto; whom no man hath seen, nor can see: to whom be honour and power everlasting. Amen."

Revelation 5:5—"Behold, the Lion of the tribe of Juda, the Root of David, hath prevailed to open the book, and to loose the seven seals thereof."

Revelation 19:16—"And he hath on his vesture and on his thigh a name written, KING OF KINGS, AND LORD OF LORDS."

Revelation 22:13, 16—"I am Alpha and Omega, the beginning and the end, the first and the last... (16) I am the root and the offspring of David, and the bright and morning star."

Quiet on the set! Take two. Back live, everybody, in three, two, one.

Pause—Listen—Reflect

* * * * * * * * *

Gargantuan Nerve

You have the gargantuan nerve! Aren't you the least bit afraid? What are you thinking? Have a drink or take a bite:

Psalm 94:7–10—"Yet they say, The Lord shall not see, neither shall the God of Jacob regard it. (8) Understand, ye brutish among the people: And ye fools, when will ye be wise? (9) He that planted the ear, shall he not hear? He that formed the eye, shall he not see? (10) He that chastiseth the heathen, shall not he correct? He that teacheth man knowledge, shall not he know?"

Isaiah 29:15, 16—"Woe unto them that seek deep to hide their counsel from the Lord, and their works are in the dark, and they say, Who seeth us? and who knoweth us? (16) Surely your turning of things upside down shall be esteemed as the potter's clay: For shall the work say of him that made it, He made me not?"

Isaiah 45:9, 10—"Woe unto him that striveth with his Maker! Let the potsherd strive with the potsherds of the earth. Shall the clay say to him that fashioneth it, What makest thou? Or thy work, He hath no hands? (10) Woe unto him that saith unto his father, What begettest thou? Or to the woman, What hast thou brought forth?"

Jeremiah 18:6—"Cannot I do with you as this potter? saith the Lord. Behold, as the clay is in the potter's hand, so are ye in mine hand..."

Romans 9:20, 21—"Nay but, O man, who art thou that repliest against God? Shall the thing formed say to him that formed it, Why hast thou made me thus? (21) Hath not the potter power over the clay, of the same lump to make one vessel unto honour, and another unto dishonour?"

If this isn't enough to make you reconsider, repent, and reassemble, nothing else will. At length, you'll be rendered heartless, just about lifeless. Have you not any fear? You've got the nerve!

Pause—Listen—Reflect

* * * * * * * *

Dead End

Where do you think you are running to? It's a dead-end path up ahead. If you continue on, you will be forced to turn around. You will still eventually wind up right back where you started. Right back at the beginning. There's no escaping. There is no other way out or around it. Have a drink or take a bite:

> Job 34:22—"There is no darkness, nor shadow of death, where the workers of iniquity may hide themselves."

> Psalm 139:7–12—"Whither shall I go from thy spirit? Or whither shall I flee from thy presence? (8) If I ascend up into heaven, thou art there: If I make my bed in hell, behold, thou art there. (9) If I take the wings of the morning, and dwell in the uttermost parts of the sea; (10) Even there shall thy hand lead me, and thy right hand shall hold me. (11) If I say, Surely the darkness shall cover me; even the night shall be light about me. (12) Yea, the darkness hideth not from thee; but the night shineth as the day: The darkness and the light are both alike to thee."

> Jeremiah 23:24—"Can any hide himself in secret places that I shall not see him? saith the Lord. Do not I fill heaven and earth? saith the Lord."

Amos 9:2–4—"Though they dig into hell, thence shall mine hand take them; though they climb up to heaven, thence will I bring them down: (3) And though they hide themselves in the top of Carmel, I will search and take them out thence; and though they be hid from my sight in the bottom of the sea, thence will I command the serpent, and he shall bite them: (4) And though they go into captivity before their enemies, thence will I command the sword, and it shall slay them: And I will set mine eyes upon them for evil, and not for good."

Hebrews 4:13—"Neither is there any creature that is not manifest in his sight: but all things are naked and opened unto the eyes of him with whom we have to do."

Yes, you can go ahead and run. Run as fast as your little feet will carry you since that is your prerogative. No one can hinder you. But as you are running, understand the rug soon will be pulled out from under you. You can run as hard and as fast as you can, but you surely cannot hide. You will never escape accountability. No, not from God.

Pause—Listen—Reflect

* * * * * * * *

Giving Up

I know it gets hard sometimes. It sure makes you feel like giving up. But before you capitulate, try what you instinctively do just as soon as you feel a migraine coming on; medicate yourself before it comes on too strong. Go ahead; give it a shot. Take a hit or maybe even two. Have a drink or take a bite:

Psalm 27:14—"Wait on the Lord: Be of good courage, and he shall strengthen thine heart: Wait, I say, on the Lord."

Psalm 31:24—"Be of good courage, and he shall strengthen your heart, all ye that hope in the Lord."

1 Corinthians 16:13—"Watch ye, stand fast in the faith, quit you like men, be strong."

2 Corinthians 12:8, 9—"For this thing I besought the Lord thrice, that it might depart from me. (9) And he said unto me, My grace is sufficient for thee: for my strength is made perfect in weakness..."

Philippians 4:13, 19—"I can do all things through Christ which strengtheneth me... (19) But my God shall supply all your need according to his riches in glory by Christ Jesus."

Ephesians 3:16—"That he would grant you, according to the riches of his glory, to be strengthened with might by his Spirit in the inner man."

Ephesians 6:10–14—"Finally, my brethren, be strong in the Lord, and in the power of his might. (11) Put on the whole armour of God, that ye may be able to stand against the wiles of the devil. (12) For we wrestle not against flesh and blood, but against principalities, against powers, against the rulers of the darkness of this world, against spiritual wickedness in high places (13) Wherefore take unto you the whole armour of God, that ye may be able to withstand in the evil day, and having done all, to stand. (14) Stand therefore..."

Are you feeling better yet? If not, take another hit, and another hit, and another hit until times get better.

Pause—Listen—Reflect

* * * * * * * * *

Winners and Champions

Somebody, anybody, please help me understand. How in the world did we manage to be crowned heavyweight champions and world-class winners without ever fighting a battle or running a race? We hadn't even gone as far as walking on a track or entering a ring. Yet we are standing on the winner's podium after only showing up at the venue. Is that it? That's all? Have a drink or take a bite:

> Ecclesiastes 9:11—"I returned, and saw under the sun, that the race is not to the swift, nor the battle to the strong..."

> Isaiah 53:11—"By his knowledge shall my righteous servant justify many; for he shall bear their iniquities."

> Matthew 1:21—"And she shall bring forth a son, and thou shalt call his name JESUS: for he shall save his people from their sins."

> Luke 2:11—"For unto you is born this day in the city of David a Saviour, which is Christ the Lord."

> John 1:29—"Behold the Lamb of God, which taketh away the sin of the world."

> Romans 5:18, 19—"Therefore as by the offence of one judgment came upon all men to condemnation;

even so by the righteousness of one the free gift came upon all men unto justification of life. (19) For as by one man's disobedience many were made sinners, so by the obedience of one shall many be made righteous."

Ephesians 4:8—"When he ascended up on high, he led captivity captive, and gave gifts unto men."

Thanks be to God. Glory to His matchless, high name. We wound up on the winner's podium on account of our Lord running the race and fighting the battle on our behalf. Hallelujah! We are hereby declared winners and champions solely because we've embraced His finished work at Calvary, regardless of what anyone else may say.

Pause—Listen—Reflect

* * * * * * * *

Help's on the Way

In the midst of going through your tribulations, you can hardly see where you are heading. Regardless, continue holding out hope. Never quit. Keep going. Your destination is just up ahead, right around the corner. You'll be surprised to know your future looks bright and dazzling. Have a drink or take a bite:

Psalm 27:13, 14—"I had fainted, unless I had believed to see the goodness of the Lord in the land of the living. (14) Wait on the Lord: Be of good courage, and he shall strengthen thine heart: Wait, I say, on the Lord."

Psalm 31:24—"Be of good courage, and he shall strengthen your heart, all ye that hope in the Lord."

Psalm 37:7, 34—"Rest in the Lord, and wait patiently for him... (34) Wait on the Lord, and keep his way, and he shall exalt thee to inherit the land..."

Psalm 40:1—"I waited patiently for the Lord; and he inclined unto me, and heard my cry."

Psalm 62:5—"My soul, wait thou only upon God; for my expectation is from him."

Psalm 130:5, 6—"I wait for the Lord, my soul doth wait, and in his word do I hope. (6) My soul waiteth for the Lord more than they that watch for the morning: I say, more than they that watch for the morning."

Habakkuk 2:3—"For the vision is yet for an appointed time, but at the end it shall speak, and not lie: Though it tarry, wait for it; because it will surely come, it will not tarry."

Acts 27:25—"Wherefore, sirs, be of good cheer: for I believe God, that it shall be even as it was told me."

Yes, keep holding out hope. Your help is on the way. The Word of the Lord will land you right at your destination. Your future looks so bright and blinding to the extent that I am beginning to get a little bit jealous of you.

Pause—Listen—Reflect

* * * * * * * *

Rising Up

Just when I thought I had it under control, I felt it rising up again just as before. Before I knew it, I got so angry my blood began to boil. I actually thought I was over it. Lord Jesus, help me, please. I am tired of reliving the hurt over and over and over again. I cannot continue to go on like this any longer. Have a drink or take a bite:

> Ecclesiastes 9:3—"This is an evil among all things that are done under the sun, that there is one event unto all: yea, also the heart of the sons of men is full of evil, and madness is in their heart while they live, and after that they go to the dead."

> Jeremiah 17:9—"The heart is deceitful above all things, and desperately wicked: who can know it?"

> Matthew 15:18–20—"But those things which proceed out of the mouth come forth from the heart; and they defile the man. (19) For out of the heart proceed evil thoughts, murders, adulteries, fornications, thefts, false witness, blasphemies: (20) These are the things which defile a man..."

> Romans 7:15, 18, 19, 24, 25—"For that which I do I allow not: for what I would, that do I not; but what I hate, that do I... (18) For I know that in me (that is, in my flesh,) dwelleth no good thing: for to will is present with me; but how to perform that which is good I find not. (19) For the good that I would I do not: but the evil which I would not, that I do... (24) O wretched man that I am! who shall deliver me from the body of this death? (25) I thank God through Jesus Christ our Lord. So then with the mind I myself serve the law of God; but with the flesh the law of sin."

> James 3:6—"And the tongue is a fire, a world of iniquity: so is the tongue among our members, that it defileth the whole body, and setteth on fire the course of nature; and it is set on fire of hell."

Thank God, through Jesus Christ, I find hope, healing, and help to break the cycle after all. All of my help comes from the Lord.

Pause—Listen—Reflect

* * * * * * * * *

Drink Up

For someone whose survival utterly depends on *acqua naturale*, surely you cannot afford not to drink up, and lots of it. Yet to a greater degree, I present to you something substantially more thirst quenching: *acqua spirituale*. Have a drink or take a bite:

> Isaiah 12:3—"Therefore with joy shall ye draw water out of the wells of salvation."

> Isaiah 44:3—"For I will pour water upon him that is thirsty, and floods upon the dry ground..."

> Isaiah 55:1, 2—"Ho, every one that thirsteth, come ye to the waters, and he that hath no money; come ye, buy, and eat; Yea, come, buy wine and milk without money and without price. (2) Wherefore do ye spend money for that which is not bread? And your labour for that which satisfieth not?"

> John 4:13, 14—"Whosoever drinketh of this water shall thirst again: (14) But whosoever drinketh of the water that I shall give him shall never thirst;

83

but the water that I shall give him shall be in him a well of water springing up into everlasting life."

John 7:37, 38—"If any man thirst, let him come unto me, and drink. (38) He that believeth on me, as the scripture hath said, out of his belly shall flow rivers of living water."

Revelation 21:6—"And he said unto me, It is done. I am Alpha and Omega, the beginning and the end. I will give unto him that is athirst of the fountain of the water of life freely."

Revelation 22:17—"And the Spirit and the bride say, Come. And let him that heareth say, Come. And let him that is athirst come. And whosoever will, let him take the water of life freely."

Come now. Drink up. Free drinks on the house for everyone; it's all on His tab, prepaid in full.

Pause—Listen—Reflect

* * * * * * * * *

Keep It Moving

Even when it appears you are not moving forward at all, keep it moving. That's called "Mark time, march!" Even when you face an invisible opponent, keep fighting. That's called shadowboxing. Even when you are not in a race, keep running. That's called training. No one ever gets ahead standing still. Keep it moving. Have a drink or take a bite:

1 Corinthians 9:24–27—"Know ye not that they which run in a race run all, but one receiveth the

prize? So run, that ye may obtain. (25) And every man that striveth for the mastery is temperate in all things. Now they do it to obtain a corruptible crown; but we an incorruptible. (26) I therefore so run, not as uncertainly; so fight I, not as one that beateth the air: (27) But I keep under my body, and bring it into subjection: lest that by any means, when I have preached to others, I myself should be a castaway."

2 Timothy 2:3–5—"Thou therefore endure hardness, as a good soldier of Jesus Christ. (4) No man that warreth entangleth himself with the affairs of this life; that he may please him who hath chosen him to be a soldier. (5) And if a man also strive for masteries, yet is he not crowned, except he strive lawfully."

2 Timothy 4:7—"I have fought a good fight, I have finished my course, I have kept the faith..."

Hebrews 12:1—"Wherefore seeing we also are compassed about with so great a cloud of witnesses, let us lay aside every weight, and the sin which doth so easily beset us, and let us run with patience the race that is set before us..."

Keep moving. Your arrival depends on it. Keep fighting. Your victory depends on it. Keep running, and fast too. Your winning depends on it.

Pause—Listen—Reflect

* * * * * * * *

End It

Put an end to *it* before *it* puts an end to you. Basta! You have had enough of it. It is high time you move on from it. Have a drink or take a bite:

> Proverbs 4:24, 25—"Put away from thee a froward mouth, and perverse lips put far from thee. (25) Let thine eyes look right on, and let thine eyelids look straight before thee."

> Ephesians 4:22–24, 31—"That ye put off concerning the former conversation the old man, which is corrupt according to the deceitful lusts; (23) And be renewed in the spirit of your mind; (24) and that ye put on the new man, which after God is created in righteousness and true holiness... (31) Let all bitterness, and wrath, and anger, and clamour, and evil speaking, be put away from you, with all malice:"

> Colossians 3:5, 8—"Mortify therefore your members which are upon the earth; fornication, uncleanness, inordinate affection, evil concupiscence, and covetousness, which is idolatry... (8) But now ye also put off all these; anger, wrath, malice, blasphemy, filthy communication out of your mouth."

> 1 Peter 2:1—"Wherefore laying aside all malice, and all guile, and hypocrisies, and envies, and all evil speakings..."

> Romans 12:2—"And be not conformed to this world: but be ye transformed by the renewing of your mind, that ye may prove what is that good, and acceptable, and perfect, will of God."

Handle *it* before *it* handles you. It's left up to you to put it to rest.

Pause—Listen—Reflect

* * * * * * * * *

Synchronized

I am immensely fascinated by line and ballroom dancing. Their synchronized, rhythmic, marvelously choreographed movements are absolutely captivating and exhilarating. *Me encanta mucho. Lo amo moltissimo. Je l'aime beaucoup.* I mean, I love it! Just love it! Have a drink or take a bite:

> Ezekiel 1:12, 16, 17, 19–21—"And they went every one straight forward: whither the spirit was to go, they went; and they turned not when they went... (16) The appearance of the wheels and their work was like unto the colour of a beryl: and they four had one likeness: and their appearance and their work was as it were a wheel in the middle of a wheel. (17) When they went, they went upon their four sides: and they turned not when they went... (19) And when the living creatures went, the wheels went by them: and when the living creatures were lifted up from the earth, the wheels were lifted up. (20) Whithersoever the spirit was to go, they went, thither was their spirit to go; and the wheels were lifted up over against them: for the spirit of the living creature was in the wheels. (21) When those went, these went; and when those stood, these stood; and when those were lifted up from the earth, the wheels were lifted up over against them: for the spirit of the living creature was in the wheels."

Ezekiel 10:10, 11, 16, 17—"And as for their appearances, they four had one likeness, as if a wheel had been in the midst of a wheel. (11) When they went, they went upon their four sides; they turned not as they went, but to the place whither the head looked they followed it; they turned not as they went... (16) And when the cherubims went, the wheels went by them: and when the cherubims lifted up their wings to mount up from the earth, the same wheels also turned not from beside them. (17) When they stood, these stood; and when they were lifted up, these lifted up themselves also: for the spirit of the living creature was in them."

What more can I say? When in step with the Spirit, it's one magnificent, remarkable, spectacular, and breathtaking sight. It is indeed one beautifully well-synchronized sight to behold.

Pause—Listen—Reflect

* * * * * * * * *

Final Result

I have finally grown to enjoy working in my yard. How did I arrive at that? I fell in love with the final result. A beautifully landscaped and eye-catching curb appeal was my incentive. There's only one thing, though: I wish I didn't have to be out in the scorching-hot sun for so long, and equally as often. Nevertheless, I'm sold on the final result. Have a drink or take a bite:

Matthew 5:12—"Rejoice, and be exceeding glad: for great is your reward in heaven... "

Romans 2:6, 7—"Who will render to every man according to his deeds: (7) To them who by patient continuance in well doing seek for glory and honour and immortality, eternal life..."

Romans 8:18—"For I reckon that the sufferings of this present time are not worthy to be compared with the glory which shall be revealed in us."

1 Corinthians 15:58—"Therefore, my beloved brethren, be ye stedfast, unmoveable, always abounding in the work of the Lord, forasmuch as ye know that your labour is not in vain in the Lord."

2 Corinthians 4:17—"For our light affliction, which is but for a moment, worketh for us a far more exceeding and eternal weight of glory."

Galatians 6:9—"And let us not be weary in well doing: for in due season we shall reap, if we faint not."

James 1:2, 3—"My brethren, count it all joy when ye fall into divers temptations; (3) Knowing this, that the trying of your faith worketh worketh patience."

James 5:7, 8—"Be patient therefore, brethren, unto the coming of the Lord. Behold, the husbandman waiteth for the precious fruit of the earth, and hath long patience for it, until he receive the early and latter rain. (8) Be ye also patient; stablish your hearts..."

1 Peter 1:6, 7—"Wherein ye greatly rejoice, though now for a season, if need be, ye are in heaviness through manifold temptations: (7) That the trial of your faith, being much more precious than of gold that perisheth, though it be tried with fire, might

be found unto praise and honour and glory at the appearing of Jesus Christ..."

1 Peter 4:12, 13—"Beloved, think it not strange concerning the fiery trial which is to try you, as though some strange thing happened unto you: (13) But rejoice, inasmuch as ye are partakers of Christ's sufferings; that, when his glory shall be revealed, ye may be glad also with exceeding joy."

Matthew 24:13—"But he that shall endure unto the end, the same shall be saved."

Your excruciating, tiresome labor and diligent continuance pay sizable dividends. The end result scores high on the proverbial Richter scale. Maintain your motivation. The final result makes it all worthwhile.

Pause—Listen—Reflect

* * * * * * * * *

Rest and Recuperate

Read this s-l-o-w-l-y all the way through. Take your time. Let this sink in deeply. Linger until it hits rock bottom. Resist the urge to rush through it. There's a refreshing outcome at the end. Rest and recuperate. Have a drink or take a bite:

Psalm 116:7—"Return unto thy rest, O my soul; for the Lord hath dealt bountifully with thee."

Isaiah 28:12—"This is the rest wherewith ye may cause the weary to rest; and this is the refreshing..."

Isaiah 30:15—"For thus saith the Lord God, the Holy One of Israel; in returning and rest shall ye be saved; in quietness and in confidence shall be your strength..."

Jeremiah 6:16—"Thus saith the Lord, Stand ye in the ways, and see, and ask for the old paths, where is the good way, and walk therein, and ye shall find rest for your souls..."

Matthew 11:28–30—"Come unto me, all ye that labour and are heavy laden, and I will give you rest. (29) Take my yoke upon you, and learn of me; for I am meek and lowly in heart: and ye shall find rest unto your souls. (30) For my yoke is easy, and my burden is light."

Hebrews 4:9–11—"There remaineth therefore a rest to the people of God. (10) For he that is entered into his rest, he also hath ceased from his own works, as God did from his. (11) Let us labour therefore to enter into that rest..."

No matter what you're confronted with right now, you will come through it—way out ahead of your adversities. Regroup, return, and relaunch.

Pause—Listen—Reflect

* * * * * * * *

All In

Win or lose, approve or disapprove, like it or not, I'm all in; in for the long haul. No doubt about it. Have a drink or take a bite:

Romans 8:38, 39—"For I am persuaded, that neither death, nor life, nor angels, nor principalities,
nor powers, nor things present, nor things to come,
(39) Nor height, nor depth, nor any other creature,
shall be able to separate us from the love of God,
which is in Christ Jesus our Lord."

Romans 14:5—"Let every man be fully persuaded
in his own mind."

2 Timothy 1:12—"Nevertheless I am not ashamed:
for I know whom I have believed, and am persuaded that he is able to keep that which I have
committed unto him against that day."

That's a wrap. It's a done deal. You can bank on it. His track record
is impeccable. That is why I'm all in.

Pause—Listen—Reflect

* * * * * * * * *

Come This Far

We didn't come this far just to come this far. No, we didn't. We
are going the full distance. Have a drink or take a bite:

1 Corinthians 9:27—"But I keep under my body,
and bring it into subjection: lest that by any means,
when I have preached to others, I myself should
be a castaway."

Hebrews 10:35–37—"Cast not away therefore
your confidence, which hath great recompence of
reward. (36) For ye have need of patience, that,
after ye have done the will of God, ye might

receive the promise. (37) For yet a little while, and he that shall come will come, and will not tarry."

Go with God, all the way. Yes, let's go the full distance. There's no giving up now. We have come too far to turn back around. Let's finish strong.

Pause—Listen—Reflect

* * * * * * * * *

Middle of the Road

I am generally a middle-of-the-road kinda guy, except where there's a mandate that requires me to choose sides. But even then, I still habitually strive to find the middle ground. Nevertheless, there are times when I'm given an ultimatum: this or that, here or over there, now or later. I recognize there are situations in which it's entirely unfeasible to have it both ways. There comes a time when it is incumbent upon you to make a choice. Have a drink or take a bite:

> Numbers 16:19–24, 26–33—"And Korah gathered all the congregation against them unto the door of the tabernacle of the congregation: and the glory of the Lord appeared unto all the congregation. (20) And the Lord spake unto Moses and unto Aaron, saying, (21) Separate yourselves from among this congregation, that I may consume them in a moment. (22) And they fell upon their faces, and said, O God, the God of the spirits of all flesh, shall one man sin, and wilt thou be wroth with all the congregation? (23) And the Lord spake unto Moses, saying, (24) Speak unto the congregation, saying, Get you up from about the tabernacle of Korah, Dathan, and Abiram... (26) And

he spake unto the congregation, saying, Depart, I pray you, from the tents of these wicked men, and touch nothing of theirs, lest ye be consumed in all their sins. (27) So they gat up from the tabernacle of Korah, Dathan, and Abiram... (28) And Moses said, Hereby ye shall know that the Lord hath sent me to do all these works; for I have not done them of mine own mind. (29) If these men die the common death of all men, or if they be visited after the visitation of all men; then the Lord hath not sent me. (30) But if the Lord make a new thing, and the earth open her mouth, and swallow them up, with all that appertain unto them, and they go down quick into the pit; then ye shall understand that these men have provoked the Lord. (31) And it came to pass, as he had made an end of speaking all these words, that the ground clave asunder that was under them: (32) And the earth opened her mouth, and swallowed them up, and their houses, and all the men that appertained unto Korah, and all their goods. (33) They, and all that appertained to them, went down alive into the pit, and the earth closed upon them: and they perished from among the congregation."

Joshua 24:15—"And if it seem evil unto you to serve the Lord, choose you this day whom ye will serve; whether the gods which your fathers served that were on the other side of the flood, or the gods of the Amorites, in whose land ye dwell: but as for me and my house, we will serve the Lord."

1 Kings 18:21—"And Elijah came unto all the people, and said, How long halt ye between two opinions? if the Lord be God, follow him: but if Baal, then follow him..."

1 Chronicles 21:10–13—"Go and tell David, saying, Thus saith the Lord, I offer thee three things: choose thee one of them, that I may do it unto thee. (11) So Gad came to David, and said unto him, Thus saith the Lord, Choose thee (12) Either three years' famine; or three months to be destroyed before thy foes, while that the sword of thine enemies overtaketh thee; or else three days the sword of the Lord, even the pestilence, in the land, and the angel of the Lord destroying throughout all the coasts of Israel. Now therefore advise thyself what word I shall bring again to him that sent me. (13) And David said unto Gad, I am in a great strait: let me fall now into the hand of the Lord; for very great are his mercies: but let me not fall into the hand of man."

Matthew 6:24—"No man can serve two masters: for either he will hate the one, and love the other; or else he will hold to the one, and despise the other. Ye cannot serve God and mammon."

I wouldn't advise you to wait until your back is up against the proverbial wall. No, not I. Never! But, rather, whenever time is of the essence, and you've run out of time, here is what I suggest: be resolute. Pick a side. Make your choice and forge ahead.

Pause—Listen—Reflect

* * * * * * * * *

Care Enough

Long after exhausting every effort to ease one's pain, and to no avail at that, keep on caring. Care enough to try and try again. Continue caring, even when it boils down to nothing more than just holding hands and shedding tears together. Since we can never really *feel* another's pain, at least, let them feel your presence way beyond just being present. That alone goes a long way. Have a drink or take a bite:

> Jeremiah 8:21, 22—"For the hurt of the daughter of my people am I hurt; I am black; astonishment hath taken hold on me. (22) Is there no balm in Gilead; is there no physician there?"

> Jeremiah 51:8—"Babylon is suddenly fallen and destroyed: Howl for her; take balm for her pain, if so be she may be healed."

> Romans 12:15—"Rejoice with them that do rejoice, and weep with them that weep."

> 1 Corinthians 12:25, 26—"That there should be no schism in the body; but that the members should have the same care one for another. (26) And whether one member suffer, all the members suffer with it; or one member be honoured, all the members rejoice with it."

A warm embrace, a gentle touch, a soft sigh—they go a very long way to soothe one's pain. Sitting there silently, in a quiet space, just the two of you, speechless, for hours on end, because you care enough. Empathy is an age-old healing balm.

Pause—Listen—Reflect

* * * * * * * * *

Coming or Going

Sometimes I just don't know if I'm coming or going, but somehow, unbeknownst to me, I always seem to end up right where I belong. How does that happen? All I can say is, have a drink or take a bite:

> Proverbs 3:5, 6—"Trust in the Lord with all thine heart; and lean not unto thine own understanding. (6) In all thy ways acknowledge him, and he shall direct thy paths."

> Psalm 37:23—"The steps of a good man are ordered by the Lord: And he delighteth in his way."

> Proverbs 16:9—"A man's heart deviseth his way: But the Lord directeth his steps."

> John 3:8—"The wind bloweth where it listeth, and thou hearest the sound thereof, but canst not tell whence it cometh, and whither it goeth: so is every one that is born of the Spirit."

Despite it all, trust God and keep it moving. Regardless of whether or not you're coming or going, maintain your trust in God and keep on persevering.

Pause—Listen—Reflect

* * * * * * * * *

Stop, Look, Listen

Stop, look, listen. Is it a bird? Is it a plane? Listen! It sounds like the voice of Robin from *Batman*. Holy no, man! It's the Lamb of God. Have a drink or take a bite:

97

John 1:29—"Look! The Lamb of God who takes away the sin of the world!" (NLT).

The fictional Superman has nothing to compare with "the Lamb of God who takes away the sin of the world." Sins past, sins present, sins future—the Lamb has triumphed over all. Stay the course with the Lamb of God.

Pause—Listen—Reflect

* * * * * * * * *

This or That

Some things you must give up so you don't give up. At other times, you just have to walk away and never look back, not even to catch one final glimpse. You cannot often have this and that. Have a drink or take a bite:

Matthew 6:24—"No man can serve two masters: for either he will hate the one, and love the other; or else he will hold to the one, and despise the other. Ye cannot serve God and mammon."

Ecclesiastes 3:1–3, 5–8—"To every thing there is a season, and a time to every purpose under the heaven: (2) A time to be born, and a time to die; a time to plant, and a time to pluck up that which is planted; (3) a time to kill, and a time to heal; a time to break down, and a time to build up... (5) a time to cast away stones, and a time to gather stones together; a time to embrace, and a time to refrain from embracing; (6) a time to get, and a time to lose; a time to keep, and a time to cast away; (7) a time to rend, and a time to sew; a time to keep silence, and a time to speak; (8) a time to love, and a time to hate; a time of war, and a time of peace."

The time has come for you to make your choice. Time's up for you having it both ways. Not even for a minute longer. Which is it going to be? This or that? Time is of the essence. Discern the time. Which is it going to be? This or that?

Pause—Listen—Reflect

* * * * * * * * *

Positive and Negative

One enormous challenge after another leads to one ginormous victory after another. Through blood, sweat, and tears, we claim our conquests. Have a drink or take a bite:

> 2 Corinthians 12:9, 10—"And he said unto me, My grace is sufficient for thee: for my strength is made perfect in weakness. Most gladly therefore will I rather glory in my infirmities, that the power of Christ may rest upon me. (10) Therefore I take pleasure in infirmities, in reproaches, in necessities, in persecutions, in distresses for Christ's sake: for when I am weak, then am I strong."

> Philippians 4:13—"For I can do everything through Christ, who gives me strength" (NLT).

Equal but opposite forces work together for the greater good. Consider a battery's positive and negative terminals. Neither yields any result without the other. Power isn't generated; no juice, unless both are operative. Don't always shun the negatives, but always gravitate toward the positives. They are both usually joined at the hip.

Pause—Listen—Reflect

* * * * * * * * *

Hammer and Nails

I know—when you're a hammer, everything looks like a nail, but wait before you start pounding away. Some things are push-pins, not nails. This isn't a one-size-fits-all or a cookie-cutter model. Look before you leap and gauge before you pound. Be deliberate, of course, but measured, even with hammer in hand. Have a drink or take a bite:

> Proverbs 11:30—"The fruit of the righteous is a tree of life; and he that winneth souls is wise."

> 1 Corinthians 3:6, 7—"I have planted, Apollos watered; but God gave the increase. (7) So then neither is he that planteth any thing, neither he that watereth; but God that giveth the increase."

> 1 Corinthians 9:19–22—"Yet have I made myself servant unto all, that I might gain the more. (20) And unto the Jews I became as a Jew, that I might gain the Jews; to them that are under the law, as under the law, that I might gain them that are under the law; (21) To them that are without law, as without law, (being not without law to God, but under the law to Christ,) that I might gain them that are without law. (22) To the weak became I as weak, that I might gain the weak: I am made all things to all men, that I might by all means save some."

Wisdom speaks: you cannot hammer away at a preteen the same as you would a young adult. The same goes for how you hammer away at a middle-ager as opposed to a golden-ager. Pay strict attention to your captive audience. Someone's destiny may be hanging in the balance.

Pause—Listen—Reflect

* * * * * * * * *

Stand Your Ground

Stand your ground by any means necessary. Defend your territory. It's your legal obligation, especially when you come under attack. Have a drink or take a bite:

> 1 Corinthians 16:13—"Watch ye, stand fast in the faith, quit you like men, be strong."

> Galatians 5:1—"Stand fast therefore in the liberty wherewith Christ hath made us free, and be not entangled again with the yoke of bondage."

> Ephesians 6:10—"Finally, my brethren, be strong in the Lord, and in the power of his might."

> 2 Thessalonians 2:15—"Therefore, brethren, stand fast, and hold the traditions which ye have been taught, whether by word, or our epistle."

There's to be no retreat, my brother. No compromise, my sister. Be resolute. We are under spiritual attack. Stand your ground.

Pause—Listen—Reflect

* * * * * * * * *

Wrong, Right

We are witnessing the abominable becoming normalized and wrong being rebranded right. We are expected to accept the unacceptable. Does this sound topsy-turvy to you? Have a drink or take a bite:

> Isaiah 5:20—"Woe unto them that call evil good, and good evil; that put darkness for light, and light for darkness..."

You may disagree to your heart's content all day long. I cannot help that. But unapologetically, regardless of your views, unless you agree with God, you are wrong, way out of bounds. I mean dead wrong!

Pause—Listen—Reflect

* * * * * * * *

Enough

I will mince no words here: enough with your sulking about pint-size appetite foes who refuse to recognize your value and worth. Look over here. Do you see us? Great. Now begin paying closer attention to your gallon-size thirsty friends over here on the right. We think the world of you. What you're serving up isn't meant to feed everyone pulling up to your table. Have a drink or take a bite:

> Matthew 7:6—"Give not that which is holy unto the dogs, neither cast ye your pearls before swine, lest they trample them under their feet, and turn again and rend you."

Mark 7:27, 28—"But Jesus said unto her, Let the children first be filled: for it is not meet to take the children's bread, and to cast it unto the dogs. (28) And she answered and said unto him, Yes, Lord: yet the dogs under the table eat of the children's crumbs."

1 Timothy 4:12, 14—"Let no man despise thy youth; but be thou an example of the believers, in word, in conversation, in charity, in spirit, in faith, in purity... (14) Neglect not the gift that is in thee, which was given thee by prophecy..."

Titus 2:15—"Let no man despise thee."

Stop fretting yourself. You are the apple of His eye (Ps. 17:8). Pay absolutely no attention to your haters over on the opposite side. Be more attentive to your supporters over here on the right. We are the ones who really and truly matter most.

Pause—Listen—Reflect

* * * * * * * * *

That One

Why are you working so hard running away from being "that one"? Wake up and recognize the fact that you are the only "one" God uniquely designed to be "that one"! Yes, you are "one" of a kind. Have a drink or take a bite:

Psalm 139:13, 14—"For thou hast possessed my reins: Thou hast covered me in my mother's womb. (14) I will praise thee; for I am fearfully and wonderfully made: Marvellous are thy works; and that my soul knoweth right well."

Be bold. Be proud of who God made you out to be. Finish whatever He gave you to perform. You can do it, all of it, through Him who gives you strength (Phil. 4:13). Do not second-guess yourself on this one. You are on the right track. Enough said; you are "that one"!

Pause—Listen—Reflect

* * * * * * * * *

Doing Great

You are getting on phenomenally while your neighbor is having it terribly bad. And that's what really matters to them right now. The question is: how can the "getting on phenomenally" aid and assist the "having it terribly bad"? Have a drink or take a bite:

> 1 Corinthians 10:24—"But the point is not to just get by. We want to live well, but our foremost efforts should be to help others live well" (MSG).

> 1 Corinthians 10:24—"Don't be concerned for your own good but for the good of others" (NLT).

> 1 Corinthians 10:24—"Let no man seek his own, but every man another's wealth."

How many ways must this be stated before we find a way to make it happen for others as it was made to happen for us?

Pause—Listen—Reflect

* * * * * * * * *

Deeper, Higher

The deeper a foundation is dug, the higher you can build. On the other hand, the shallower the depth, the easier it comes tumbling down. Have a drink or take a bite:

> Matthew 7:24–27—"Therefore whosoever heareth these sayings of mine, and doeth them, I will liken him unto a wise man, which built his house upon a rock: (25) And the rain descended, and the floods came, and the winds blew, and beat upon that house; and it fell not: for it was founded upon a rock. (26) And every one that heareth these sayings of mine, and doeth them not, shall be likened unto a foolish man, which built his house upon the sand: (27) And the rain descended, and the floods came, and the winds blew, and beat upon that house; and it fell: and great was the fall of it."

If you aim to last, dig deep. Really deep! Before laying the very first brick, traverse a long ways down. Then you will be ready to commence building something that will last.

Pause—Listen—Reflect

* * * * * * * *

Ups and Downs

I've been up and I've been down. I have had some good days as well as some bad days. But through it all, delightfully enough, I have come to realize what was occurring the whole while. Have a drink or take a bite:

105

Romans 8:28—"And we know that all things work together for good to those who love God, to those who are the called according to His purpose."

In the end, all of my ups far outweigh my downs. All of my good days outlast my bad days. This is what I've come to realize. Everything was working for my good.

Pause—Listen—Reflect

* * * * * * * * *

Snake

Watch out! That looks like a snake. Proceed with caution, but at your own risk. Nothing good comes from you and a snake crossing paths. Have a drink or take a bite:

Genesis 3:1—"Now the serpent was more subtil than any beast of the field which the Lord God had made. And he said unto the woman, Yea, hath God said, Ye shall not eat of every tree of the garden?"

John 10:10—"The thief cometh not, but for to steal, and to kill, and to destroy..."

John 8:44—"He has always hated the truth, because there is no truth in him. When he lies, it is consistent with his character; for he is a liar and the father of lies" (NLT).

1 Peter 5:8—"Be sober, be vigilant; because your adversary the devil, as a roaring lion, walketh about, seeking whom he may devour..."

1 Peter 5:8—"Keep a cool head. Stay alert. The devil is poised to pounce, and would like nothing better than to catch you napping" (MSG).

That serpent is a schemer. He must never be trusted. Stay alert so you don't cross paths.

Pause—Listen—Reflect

* * * * * * * * *

Fight

Fight against me, and you just might stand a fighting chance. Fight against God if you dare, and you'll be finished! Have a drink or take a bite:

Acts 9:5—"I am Jesus whom thou persecutest: it is hard for thee to kick against the pricks."

You'll be finished, I say. Ruthlessly shellacked!

Pause—Listen—Reflect

* * * * * * * * *

Without

Seriously? You want to be paid without having done the work? You actually believe you will succeed without ever trying? Are you expecting answered prayers when you haven't even prayed the Lord's Prayer? Now you're wondering why nothing's working in your favor. Here's what you should do. Try this on for size. Have a drink or take a bite:

Matthew 7:7, 8—"Keep on asking, and you will receive what you ask for. Keep on seeking, and you will find. keep on knocking, and the door will be opened to you. (8) For everyone who asks, receives. Everyone who seeks, finds. And to everyone who knocks, the door will be opened" (NLT).

Hebrews 11:6—"But without faith it is impossible to please him: for he that cometh to God must believe that he is, and that he is a rewarder of them that diligently seek him."

2 Thessalonians 3:10–12—"Don't you remember the rule we had when we lived with you? "If you don't work, you don't eat." And now we're getting reports that a bunch of lazy good-for-nothings are taking advantage of you. This must not be tolerated. We command them to get to work immediately—no excuses, no arguments—and earn their own keep" (MSG).

Nothing from nothing leaves absolutely nothing. Nothing plus nothing still yields the selfsame result: nothing! You gotta have somethin'. You get my drift?

Pause—Listen—Reflect

* * * * * * * *

No Eraser

Real life has no eraser. It's written permanently with indelible ink. Be careful how you write, draw, make notes, jot things down, or even scribble with it. Have a drink or take a bite:

Matthew 12:36, 37—"But I say unto you, That every idle word that men shall speak, they shall give account thereof in the day of judgment. (37) For by thy words thou shalt be justified, and by thy words thou shalt be condemned."

Romans 14:11, 12—"For it is written, As I live, saith the Lord, every knee shall bow to me, and every tongue shall confess to God. (12) So then every one of us shall give account of himself to God."

2 Corinthians 5:10—"For we must all appear before the judgment seat of Christ; that every one may receive the things done in his body, according to that he hath done, whether it be good or bad."

1 Peter 4:5—"Who shall give account to him that is ready to judge the quick and the dead."

This covers only half the story. The better half lies in the fact that, after all we've written, drawn, jotted down, and scribbled with our lives, the blood of Christ makes it good again.

Psalm 103:8–14—"The Lord is merciful and gracious, slow to anger, and plenteous in mercy. (9) He will not always chide: Neither will he keep his anger for ever. (10) He hath not dealt with us after our sins; nor rewarded us according to our iniquities. (11) For as the heaven is high above the earth, so great is his mercy toward them that fear him. (12) As far as the east is from the west, so far hath he removed our transgressions from us. (13) Like as a father pitieth his children, so the Lord pitieth them that fear him. (14) For he knoweth our frame; he remembereth that we are dust."

John 1:29—"Behold the Lamb of God, which taketh away the sin of the world."

Hebrews 9:12–14—"Neither by the blood of goats and calves, but by his own blood he entered in once into the holy place, having obtained eternal redemption for us. (13) For if the blood of bulls and of goats, and the ashes of an heifer sprinkling the unclean, sanctifieth to the purifying of the flesh: (14) How much more shall the blood of Christ, who through the eternal Spirit offered himself without spot to God, purge your conscience from dead works to serve the living God?"

That's right. Real life has no eraser, but the blood of the Lamb takes exception to that fact. The blood is more potent than the fullers' soap (Mal. 3:2). Once applied, it's as though you were never soiled. I suspect *Mr. Clean Magic Eraser* attempts to mimic this feat, but only the blood of Jesus cleanses all sin.

Pause—Listen—Reflect

* * * * * * * * *

Best and Worse

What is best for me may be worse for you. What is best for you may be worse for me. We both must compromise in order to achieve anything remotely close to being what is best for both of us. I must concede a little. You must concede a little. That's how this works. Have a drink or take a bite:

Philippians 2:3, 4—"Let nothing be done through strife or vainglory; but in lowliness of mind let each esteem other better than themselves. (4) Look not every man on his own things, but every man also on the things of others."

Philippians 2:3, 4—"If you care—then do me a favor: agree with each other, love each other, be deep-spirited friends. Don't push your way to the front; don't sweet-talk your way to the top. Put yourself aside, and help others get ahead. Don't be obsessed with getting your own advantage. Forget yourselves long enough to lend a helping hand" (MSG).

Reject the notion of playing hardball. Instead, let's work toward a general consensus just this once. Can we? Then and only then will we have it—not my way or your way, but, rather, we will have it our way.

Pause—Listen—Reflect

* * * * * * * *

Commonality

Morning, noon, night; good, better, best; one, two, three; A, B, C. Can you identify the commonalities here? Have a drink or take a bite:

Ecclesiastes 11:1—"Cast thy bread upon the waters: for thou shalt find it after many days."

Mark 4:28, 29, 31, 32—"For the earth bringeth forth fruit of herself; first the blade, then the ear, after that the full corn in the ear. (29) But when the fruit is brought forth, immediately he putteth in the sickle, because the harvest is come... (31) It is like a grain of mustard seed, which, when it is sown in the earth, is less than all the seeds that be in the earth: (32) But when it is sown, it groweth up, and becometh greater than all herbs, and shooteth out great branches; so that the fowls of the air may lodge under the shadow of it."

John 12:24—"Verily, verily, I say unto you, Except a corn of wheat fall into the ground and die, it abideth alone: but if it die, it bringeth forth much fruit."

1 Corinthians 14:40—"Let all things be done decently and in order."

Luke 6:38—"Give, and it shall be given unto you; good measure, pressed down, and shaken together, and running over, shall men give into your bosom. For with the same measure that ye mete withal it shall be measured to you again."

Were you able to identify the commonalities? If not, let me assist: there's a progressive order of things, in a sequential pattern. Nothing in, nothing out; garbage in, garbage out; seed in the ground; the harvest's on its way. It's a simple fundamental principle: seedtime and harvest. It's simple. Not complicated at all.

Pause—Listen—Reflect

* * * * * * * * *

Look

Look to the left. Look to the right. Look up. Now look down. Did you notice something? What didn't you see while you were looking around? Have a drink or take a bite:

Proverbs 4:25–27—"Let thine eyes look right on, and let thine eyelids look straight before thee. (26) Ponder the path of thy feet, and let all thy ways be established. (27) Turn not to the right hand nor to the left: Remove thy foot from evil."

Luke 17:23—"And they shall say to you, See here; or, see there: go not after them, nor follow them."

Have you recognized what you couldn't see while occupied doing recon? Let me help you. As you glanced around, it was impossible for you to maintain focus on what's in front of you. Even if but for just an instant, you lost sight of your destination. Refuse to become sidetracked. Keep looking straight forward. Stay the course. Full speed ahead.

Pause—Listen—Reflect

* * * * * * * * *

Speak

Speak up. Speak out. Be unapologetic. Do not be silent. No, not now. Have a drink or take a bite:

Matthew 10:27—"What I tell you now in the darkness, shout abroad when daybreak comes. What I whisper in your ear, shout from the housetops for all to hear!" (NLT).

1 Corinthians 14:10—"There are, it may be, so many kinds of voices in the world, and none of them is without signification."

Your voice matters. It's of great value. Use it. Refuse to be silenced.

Pause—Listen—Reflect

* * * * * * * * *

Not Alone

If you are there feeling lonely, you must know: you're not alone. No, you are not alone. We are all in this together, and we will make it through together. How do I know this? Have a drink or take a bite:

> Deuteronomy 31:6, 8—"Be strong and of a good courage, fear not, nor be afraid of them: for the Lord thy God, he it is that doth go with thee; he will not fail thee, nor forsake thee... (8) And the Lord, he it is that doth go before thee; he will be with thee, he will not fail thee, neither forsake thee: fear not, neither be dismayed."

> Matthew 28:20—"And be sure of this: I am with you always, even to the end of the age" (NLT).

Yes, that's right! No, you are not alone. God will take care of you. We have His Word on it.

Pause—Listen—Reflect

* * * * * * * * *

Brave

Get up! Stand up! No warrior wins a battle taking it lying down. Stay in the fight. You will win. Have a drink or take a bite:

Joshua 1:9—"Have not I commanded thee? Be strong and of a good courage; be not afraid, neither be thou dismayed: for the Lord thy God is with thee whithersoever thou goest."

1 Samuel 4:9—"Be strong, and quit yourselves like men...quit yourselves like men, and fight."

1 Samuel 30:8—"And David inquired at the Lord, saying, Shall I pursue after this troop? Shall I overtake them? And he answered him, Pursue: for thou shalt surely overtake them, and without fail recover all."

1 Corinthians 15:58—"Therefore, my beloved brethren, be ye stedfast, unmoveable, always abounding in the work of the Lord, forasmuch as ye know that your labour is not in vain in the Lord."

1 Corinthians 16:13—"Watch ye, stand fast in the faith, quit you like men, be strong."

Galatians 6:9—"And let us not be weary in well doing: for in due season we shall reap, if we faint not."

We are running a race that is more like a marathon than a sprint. That's why we must keep at it. Don't faint. Take a moment. Catch your breath and regroup. Now, be brave. Be resilient. Be steadfast and courageous. Go ahead; fight on. Yes, keep at it, all the way until the whistle blows, the bell rings, or the opponent taps out.

Pause—Listen—Reflect

* * * * * * * *

Certitude

In times of uncertainty, certitude in the God of time and seasons is paramount. This is no time for floundering. Have a drink or take a bite:

> Psalm 23:6—"Surely goodness and mercy shall follow me all the days of my life: And I will dwell in the house of the Lord for ever."

> Psalm 91:3, 4—"Surely he shall deliver thee from the snare of the fowler, and from the noisome pestilence. (4) He shall cover thee with his feathers, and under his wings shalt thou trust: His truth shall be thy shield and buckler."

> Hebrews 6:19—"Which hope we have as an anchor of the soul, both sure and stedfast... "

Certainly you can trust God! Long after times and seasons have passed—unquestionable, you can be sure—God will be forever by your side. He will never let you down. Of this I am certain, "both sure and steadfast."

Pause—Listen—Reflect

* * * * * * * *

No Turning Back

There is just no turning back now. We are steeped too deep and in over our heads. As a matter of fact, where would we go, anyway? Have a drink or take a bite:

> Psalm 139:7–11—"Whither shall I go from thy spirit? Or whither shall I flee from thy presence?

(8) If I ascend up into heaven, thou art there: If I make my bed in hell, behold, thou art there. (9) If I take the wings of the morning... (10) even there shall thy hand lead me, and thy right hand shall hold me. (11) If I say, Surely the darkness shall cover me; even the night shall be light about me."

John 6:67–69—"Then said Jesus unto the twelve, Will ye also go away? (68) Then Simon Peter answered him, Lord, to whom shall we go? Thou hast the words of eternal life. (69) And we believe and are sure that thou art that Christ, the Son of the living God."

It's a done deal. We have long passed the point of no return; end of discussion! Onward, Christian soldiers! March onward.

Pause—Listen—Reflect

* * * * * * * *

Hardest Fights

The hardest fights to fight are the fights we must fight the hardest. Have a drink or take a bite:

1 Timothy 6:12—"Fight the good fight of faith, lay hold on eternal life, whereunto thou art also called, and hast professed a good profession before many witnesses."

2 Timothy 4:7—"I have fought a good fight, I have finished my course, I have kept the faith."

Choose your fights wisely, even though some fights choose you. Once you've entered the ring, never stop landing blows. Dismiss every thought of giving up. Give in under no circumstances, not even for one moment. Fight the good fight.

Pause—Listen—Reflect

* * * * * * * * *

A Little

I give a little and you take a little. Then I take a little while you give a little. This is how an impermeable support system works. I support you, you support me, and we support each other. This ensures we make it through together. No one gets left behind. Have a drink or take a bite:

> Proverbs 3:27, 28—"Withhold not good from them to whom it is due, when it is in the power of thine hand to do it. (28) Say not unto thy neighbour, Go, and come again, and to morrow I will give; when thou hast it by thee."

> Luke 6:31—"Here is a simple rule of thumb for behavior: Ask yourself what you want people to do for you; then grab the initiative and do it for them!" (MSG).

> Luke 6:38—"Give, and it shall be given unto you; good measure, pressed down, and shaken together, and running over, shall men give into your bosom. For with the same measure that ye mete withal it shall be measured to you again."

> Ecclesiastes 11:1—"Send your grain across the seas, and in time, profits will flow back to you" (NLT).

Colossians 3:17—"And whatever you do or say, do it as a representative of the Lord Jesus, giving thanks through Him to God the Father" (NLT).

Offer up your little, and watch it return right back to you with interest. That's called a boomerang.

Pause—Listen—Reflect

* * * * * * * * *

Nothing

Sine qua non (without this, nothing)! Absolutely nothing! Have a drink or take a bite:

John 15:5—"Without me ye can do nothing."

Acts 4:12—"Salvation comes no other way; no other name has been or will be given to us by which we can be saved, only this one" (MSG).

Without Christ, we have nothing, positively nothing at all. If you haven't already, you should get on board.

Pause—Listen—Reflect

* * * * * * * * *

Gehenna

Are you currently going through Gehenna? If you are, don't stop in the middle of it. Keep going. You will get through it so long as you keep walking in the Light. Have a drink or take a bite:

John 8:12—"I am the light of the world: he that followeth me shall not walk in darkness, but shall have the light of life."

1 Thessalonians 5:5—"Ye are all the children of light, and the children of the day: we are not of the night, nor of darkness."

Light shines brightest in the dark. Jesus is that Light, the Light which lights up your world, even in the midst of all Gehenna. He will lead you through it. Just keep going. Never stop.

Pause—Listen—Reflect

* * * * * * * * *

Tactical

I recently learned of "tactical patience" and "tactical silence." Could these possibly be our current holding patterns? Have a drink or take a bite:

Exodus 14:13—"Don't be afraid. Just stand still and watch the Lord rescue you today..." (NLT).

Ruth 3:18—"Sit back and relax, my dear daughter, until we find out how things turn out..." (MSG).

Psalm 37:7—"Be still in the presence of the Lord, and wait patiently for him to act. Don't worry..." (NLT).

Psalm 46:10—"Be still, and know that I am God..."

Reject the notion that time spent patiently waiting in silence is time wasted. Instead, while you wait, employ prayer and praise and watch God work things out for you. Embrace this timely, purposeful tactic: patience and silence.

Pause—Listen—Reflect

* * * * * * * * *

Brighter Days

Brothers and sisters, brighter days are ahead. We haven't seen anything yet. It's going to be like nothing we've ever seen or experienced before. Have a drink or take a bite:

> Haggai 2:9—"This temple is going to end up far better than it started out, a glorious beginning but an even more glorious finish: a place in which I will hand out wholeness and holiness..." (MSG).

> 2 Chronicles 7:1, 2—"And the glory of the Lord filled the house. (2) And the priests could not enter into the house of the Lord, because the glory of the Lord had filled the Lord's house."

> Psalm 118:22, 23—"The stone which the builders refused is become the head stone of the corner. (23) This is the Lord's doing; it is marvellous in our eyes."

There are brighter days ahead, my brethren and sistren. Stay the course. Your life is on the verge of a grandiose turnaround. You are about to enter a brand-new dimension.

Pause—Listen—Reflect

* * * * * * * * *

Sssstart

Sssstart something small somewhere soon. Isn't that how the early church got its start? Since then, the rest is history; all from just one simple, small start. Have a drink or take a bite:

> Matthew 18:20—"For where two or three are gathered together in my name, there am I in the midst of them."

> Mark 6:7—"And he called unto him the twelve, and began to send them forth by two and two; and gave them power over unclean spirits;"

> Romans 16:5—"Likewise greet the church that is in their house..."

> 1 Corinthians 16:19—"Aquila and Priscilla salute you much in the Lord, with the church that is in their house."

> Colossians 4:15—"Salute the brethren which are in Laodicea, and Nymphas, and the church which is in his house."

> Philemon 2—"And to our beloved Apphia, and Archippus our fellowsoldier, and to the church in thy house."

Don't sweat it. Start right where you are, even with the teensy-weensy bit you have. Never despise small beginnings. It's not the size that matters. Go ahead. Get started. Leave the outcome to God.

Pause—Listen—Reflect

* * * * * * * *

Listen

It suddenly dawned on me not very long ago. Wow! We should listen carefully, twice as much, before we speak. That's why we are blessed with two ears but only one mouth. Have a drink or take a bite:

> Ecclesiastes 5:1, 2—"As you enter the house of God, keep your ears open and your mouth shut. It is evil to make mindless offerings to God. (2) Don't make rash promises, and don't be hasty in bringing matters before God. After all, God is in heaven, and you are here on earth. So let your words be few" (NLT).

> Proverbs 17:27, 28—"A truly wise person uses few words; a person with understanding is even-tempered. (28) Even fools are thought wise when they keep silent; with their mouths shut, they seem intelligent" (NLT).

> James 1:19—"Let every man be swift to hear, slow to speak..."

This being the case, we should listen keenly, twice as much, before running off at the mouth. You'll be thought wise. Sshhh. Shush. Hush. Listen.

Pause—Listen—Reflect

* * * * * * * *

Opposites

The quickest way up is down. One sure way to receive is to give. The proof of your strength lies in your weakness. None of this makes any sense whatsoever. Not at first glance, anyway. Not until we ponder this. Have a drink or take a bite:

> Isaiah 55:8, 9—"For my thoughts are not your thoughts, neither are your ways my ways, saith the Lord. (9) For as the heavens are higher than the earth, so are my ways higher than your ways, and my thoughts than your thoughts."

> 2 Corinthians 12:10—"And so the weaker I get, the stronger I become" (MSG).

If you haven't already learned this lesson, you haven't lived long enough yet. I implore you, keep living. You will soon be enlightened.

Pause—Listen—Reflect

* * * * * * * * *

Truth and Lies

What's right or wrong has absolutely nothing to do with whether or not we like or dislike, agree or disagree with each other. The same goes for truths and lies. Have a drink or take a bite:

> Proverbs 23:23—"Buy the truth, and sell it not..."

> Romans 3:4—"Let God be true, but every man a liar..."

124

Right is right and wrong is wrong, regardless of the status of our relationships. Love the right and hate the wrong. And while you're at it, cling to the truth but detach yourself from the lies.

Pause—Listen—Reflect

* * * * * * * * *

Do and Say

After all that's been said and done, let's not be found guilty of having said far more than we have done. Be fervent in prayer and diligent in action. Have a drink or take a bite:

> Ecclesiastes 9:10—"Whatsoever thy hand findeth to do, do it with thy might; for there is no work, nor device, nor knowledge, nor wisdom, in the grave..."

> James 2:20—"But wilt thou know, O vain man, that faith without works is dead?"

> James 5:16—"The effectual fervent prayer of a righteous man availeth much."

As the power of a hot rod lies beneath the hood, so, too, the power behind your words and actions is energized by your prayer life. Notwithstanding, given all the attention muscle cars' speed attracts, not many give a hoot about what's under the hood. Neither do many pay any attention whatsoever to your prayer life. What intrigues most about the speedster is its speed. Likewise, what primarily captivates others about you is what you say and do. That is what's most dazzling. Regardless, the hot rod's engine better be turbocharged and your prayer life best be supercharged. Lacking these, all that remain are empty shells, a beauty to behold on the outside but lackluster on the inside. Yes, graveyard dead. So put your money where your mouth is.

Pause—Listen—Reflect

* * * * * * * * *

Blessed

"How are you able to afford such niceties?" they asked. "Wow! You are really blessed. I can only dream of living as affluently as you. How did you do it?" Inquiring minds want to know. Have a drink or take a bite:

> Deuteronomy 15:10—"Thou shalt surely give him, and thine heart shall not be grieved when thou givest unto him: because that for this thing the Lord thy God shall bless thee in all thy works, and in all that thou puttest thine hand unto."

> Deuteronomy 28:2–8—"And all these blessings shall come on thee, and overtake thee, if thou shalt hearken unto the voice of the Lord thy God. (3) Blessed shalt thou be in the city, and blessed shalt thou be in the field. (4) Blessed shall be the fruit of thy body, and the fruit of thy ground, and the fruit of thy cattle, the increase of thy kine, and the flocks of thy sheep. (5) Blessed shall be thy basket and thy store. (6) Blessed shalt thou be when thou comest in, and blessed shalt thou be when thou goest out. (7) The Lord shall cause thine enemies that rise up against thee to be smitten before thy face: they shall come out against thee one way, and flee before thee seven ways. (8) The Lord shall command the blessing upon thee in thy storehouses,

and in all that thou settest thine hand unto; and he shall bless thee..."

Proverbs 3:9, 10—"Honour the Lord with thy substance, and with the firstfruits of all thine increase: (10) So shall thy barns be filled with plenty, and thy presses shall burst out with new wine."

Malachi 3:10—"Bring ye all the tithes into the storehouse, that there may be meat in mine house, and prove me now herewith, saith the Lord of hosts, if I will not open you the windows of heaven, and pour you out a blessing, that there shall not be room enough to receive it."

Luke 6:38—"Give, and it shall be given unto you; good measure, pressed down, and shaken together, and running over, shall men give into your bosom. For with the same measure that ye mete withal it shall be measured to you again."

Yes, they are correct. And we make no apologies. We are blessed. No, it didn't come easily. We sacrificed a whole lot. Our families went lacking on many occasions. But we chose to stay the course despite of it all. It isn't that we are any more favored than anyone else. No, we are not. It is possible for others to enjoy the selfsame blessings. Only do as we do. Open your hands and heart and give!

Pause—Listen—Reflect

* * * * * * * * *

Sides

Here is a tall glass of water for you. A trigon has three sides. A tetragon has four sides, a pentagon five sides, a hexagon six sides, a heptagon seven sides, an octagon eight sides, a nonagon nine sides, a decagon ten sides, a hendecagon eleven sides, a dodecagon twelve sides, a triskaidecagon thirteen sides, a tetrakaidecagon fourteen sides, a pentadecagon fifteen sides, a hexadecagon sixteen sides, a heptadecagon seventeen sides, an octadecagon eighteen sides, and an enneadecagon nineteen sides. And get this—an icosagon has twenty sides.

This truly is astounding. Not even I knew there were so many named sides. I hope I didn't lose you at around number nine, but thanks for sticking with me up to this point. Anyway, here's my central objective; this is what I am really attempting to get at: I am trying to get to the bottom of how many sides God has. Have a drink or take a bite:

> Exodus 19:9—"Behold, I come to you in the thick cloud..." (NKJV).

> Judges 13:6—"A Man of God came to me, and His countenance was like the countenance of the Angel of God, very awesome..." (NKJV).

> Psalm 46:6, 8, 9—"The nations raged, the kingdoms were moved; He uttered His voice, the earth melted... (8) Come, behold the works of the Lord, who has made desolations in the earth. (9) He makes wars cease to the end of the earth; He breaks the bow and cuts the spear in two; He burns the chariot in the fire" (NKJV).

> Psalm 50:3—"Our God shall come, and shall not keep silent; a fire shall devour before Him, and it shall be very tempestuous all around Him" (NKJV).

> Psalm 97:2–6—"Clouds and darkness surround Him; righteousness and justice are the foundation of His throne. (3) A fire goes before Him, and

burns up His enemies round about. (4) His light-
nings light the world; the earth sees and trembles.
(5) The mountains melt like wax at the presence of
the Lord, at the presence of the Lord of the whole
earth. (6) The heavens declare His righteousness,
and all the peoples see His glory" (NKJV).

Psalm 104:1–9—"O Lord my God, You are very
great: You are clothed with honor and majesty, (2)
who cover Yourself with light as with a garment,
who stretch out the heavens like a curtain. (3) He
lays the beams of His upper chambers in the waters,
who makes the clouds His chariot, who walks on
the wings of the wind, (4) Who makes His angels
spirits, His ministers a flame of fire. (5) You who
laid the foundations of the earth, so that it should
not be moved forever, (6) You covered it with the
deep as with a garment; the waters stood above
the mountains. (7) At Your rebuke they fled; at
the voice of Your thunder they hastened away. (8)
They went up over the mountains; they went down
into the valleys, to the place which You founded
for them. (9) You have set a boundary that they
may not pass over..." (NKJV).

Isaiah 66:15, 16—"For behold, the Lord will come
with fire and with His chariots, like a whirlwind,
to render His anger with fury, and His rebuke with
flames of fire. (16) For by fire and by His sword
the Lord will judge all flesh..." (NKJV).

Daniel 7:9, 10—"And the Ancient of Days was
seated; His garment was white as snow, and the
hair of His head was like pure wool. His throne
was a fiery flame, its wheels a burning fire; (10)
a fiery stream issued and came forth from before
Him..." (NKJV).

Daniel 10:5, 6—"I lifted my eyes and looked, and behold, a certain man clothed in linen, whose waist was girded with gold of Uphaz! (6) His body was like beryl, his face like the appearance of lightning, his eyes like torches of fire, his arms and feet like burnished bronze in color, and the sound of his words like the voice of a multitude" (NKJV).

Micah 1:3, 4—"For behold, the Lord is coming out of His place; He will come down and tread on the high places of the earth. (4) The mountains will melt under Him, and the valleys will split like wax before the fire, like waters poured down a steep place" (NKJV).

Nahum 1:3–5—"The Lord has His way in the whirlwind and in the storm, and the clouds are the dust of His feet. (4) He rebukes the sea and makes it dry, and dries up all the rivers. Bashan and Carmel wither, and the flower of Lebanon wilts. (5) The mountains quake before Him, the hills melt, and the earth heaves at His presence, yes, the world and all who dwell in it" (NKJV).

Mark 9:2, 3—"And He was transfigured before them. (3) His clothes became shining, exceedingly white, like snow, such as no launderer on earth can whiten them" (NKJV).

Revelation 1:13–18—"And in the midst of the seven lampstands One like the Son of Man, clothed with a garment down to the feet and girded about the chest with a golden band. (14) His head and hair were white like wool, as white as snow, and His eyes like a flame of fire; (15) His feet were like fine brass, as if refined in a furnace, and His voice as the sound of many waters; (16) ...out of

His mouth went a sharp two-edged sword, and His countenance was like the sun shining in its strength... (17) But He laid His right hand on me, saying to me, 'Do not be afraid; I am the First and the Last. (18) I am He who lives, and was dead, and behold, I am alive forevermore. Amen. And I have the keys of Hades and of Death'" (NKJV).

Revelation 19:12, 16—"His eyes were like a flame of fire, and on His head were many crowns. He had a name written that no one knew except Himself... (16) He has on His robe and on His thigh a name written: KING OF KINGS AND LORD OF LORDS" (NKJV).

Revelation 22:13, 16—"I am the Alpha and the Omega, the Beginning and the End, the First and the Last... (16) I am the Root and the Offspring of David, the Bright and Morning Star" (NKJV).

And still this hasn't even begun to scratch the surface. There are just too many sides to pursue. Continuing any further is pointless. It would be like going down the rabbit hole. Suffice it to say, we'll reasonably deduce that He is the infinite, unfathomable-sided God.

Pause—Listen—Reflect

* * * * * * * * *

Choices

Choices, choices, choices, and more choices. Good or evil? Life or death? Left or right? Up or down? Here or there? So many choices. Which should I choose? Have a drink or take a bite:

Deuteronomy 30:15, 19—"See, I have set before thee this day life and good, and death and evil... (19) I call heaven and earth to record this day against you, that I have set before you life and death, blessing and cursing: therefore choose life, that both thou and thy seed may live..."

Seriously consider the pros and cons before making your choice. It's entirely up to you which choice you make. But if I were you, I'd choose life. Hint! Hint!

Just my little two cents' worth? The choices and decisions you make today determine your tomorrow's profits or losses. I'm just saying.

Pause—Listen—Reflect

* * * * * * * * *

Adversities

I have been traumatized, hamstrung, just about tranquilized by so many of life's adversities. Like a leaky faucet, setback after setback, one blow followed by another. I've had misfortunes galore, with much more to spare. They just kept on dripping and dropping. It seemed things would never let up. But little did I know, in the thick of it, look who I discovered at the helm, orchestrating it all. Have a drink or take a bite:

Job 1:1, 3, 6, 8, 9, 11, 12, 20–22—"There was a man in the land of Uz, whose name was Job; and that man was blameless and upright, and one who feared God and shunned evil. (3) ...so that this man was the greatest of all the people of the East... (6) Now there was a day when the sons of God came to present themselves before the Lord, and Satan

132

also came among them... (8) Then the Lord said to Satan, 'Have you considered my servant Job, that there is none like him on the earth, a blameless and upright man, one who fears God and shuns evil?' (9) So Satan answered the Lord and said, 'Does Job fear God for nothing?... (11) But now, stretch out Your hand and touch all that he has, and he will surely curse You to Your face!' (12) And the Lord said to Satan, 'Behold, all that he has is in your power; only do not lay a hand on his person...' (20) Then Job arose, tore his robe, and shaved his head; and he fell to the ground and worshiped. (21) And he said: 'Naked I came from my mother's womb, and naked shall I return there. The Lord gave, and the Lord has taken away; blessed be the name of the Lord.' (22) In all this Job did not sin nor charge God with wrong..." (NKJV).

Job 2:3–10—"Then the Lord said to Satan, 'Have you considered My servant Job, that there is none like him on the earth, a blameless and upright man, one who fears God and shuns evil? And still he holds fast to his integrity, although you incited Me against him, to destroy him without cause.' (4) So Satan answered the Lord and said, 'Skin for skin! Yes, all that a man has he will give for his life. (5) But stretch out Your hand now, and touch his bone and his flesh, and he will surely curse You to Your face!' (6) And the Lord said to Satan, 'Behold, he is in your hand, but spare his life.' (7) So Satan went out from the presence of the Lord, and struck Job with painful boils from the sole of his foot to the crown of his head. (8) And he took for himself a potsherd with which to scrape himself while he sat in the midst of the ashes. (9) Then his wife said to him, 'Do you still hold fast to your integrity? Curse God and die!' (10) But he said to her, 'You speak as one of the foolish women speaks. Shall we indeed accept good from God, and shall we not accept adversity?' In all this Job did not sin with his lips" (NKJV).

Job 3:1–12, 16, 20, 21, 23–26—"After this Job opened his mouth and cursed the day of his birth. (2) And Job spoke, and said: (3) 'May the day perish on which I was born, and the night in which it was said, "A male child is conceived." (4) May that day be darkness...nor the light shine upon it. (5) May darkness and the shadow of death claim it; may a cloud settle on it; may the blackness of the day terrify it. (6) As for that night, may darkness seize it; may it not rejoice among the days of the year, may it not come into the number of the months. (7) Oh, may that night be barren! May no joyful shout come into it! (8) May those curse it who curse the day... (9) May the stars of its morning be dark; may it look for light, but have none, and not see the dawning of the day; (10) because it did not shut up the doors of my mother's womb, nor hide sorrow from my eyes. (11) Why did I not die at birth? Why did I not perish when I came from the womb? (12) Why did the knees receive me? Or why the breasts, that I should nurse?... (16) Or why was I not hidden like a stillborn child, like infants who never saw light?... (20) Why is light given to him who is in misery, and life to the bitter of soul, (21) who long for death, but it does not come... (23) Why is light given to a man whose way is hidden, and whom God has hedged in? (24) For my sighing comes before I eat, and my groanings pour out like water. (25) For the thing I greatly feared has come upon me, and what I dreaded has happened to me. (26) I am not at ease, nor am I quiet; I have no rest, for trouble comes'" (NKJV).

Job 19:8–21, 25–27—"He has fenced up my way, so that I cannot pass; and He has set darkness in my paths. (9) He has stripped me of my glory, and taken the crown from my mead. (10) He breaks me down on every side, and I am gone; my hope He has uprooted like a tree. (11) He has also kindled His wrath against me, and He counts me as one of His enemies. (12) His troops come together and build up their road against me; they encamp all around my tent. (13) He has removed my brothers far from me, and my acquaintances are completely estranged from me. (14) My relatives have failed, and my close friends have forgotten me. (15) Those who dwell in my house, and my maidservants, count me as a stranger; I am an alien in their sight. (16) I call my servant, but he gives no answer... (17) My breath is offensive to my wife, and I am repulsive to the children of my own body. (18) Even young children despise me; I arise, and they speak against me. (19) All my close friends abhor me, and those whom I love have turned against me. (20) My bone clings to my skin and to my flesh, and I have escaped by the skin of my teeth. (21) Have pity on me, have pity on me, O you my friends, for the hand of God has struck me!... (25) For I know that my Redeemer lives, and He shall stand at last on the earth; (26) and after my skin is destroyed, this I know, that in my flesh I shall see God, (27) whom I shall see for myself, and my eyes shall behold, and not another. How my heart yearns within me!" (NKJV).

Job 23:8–12—"Look, I go forward, but He is not there, and backward, but I cannot perceive Him; (9) When He works on the left hand, I cannot behold Him; when He turns to the right hand, I cannot see Him. (10) But He knows the way that I take; when He has tested me, I shall come forth as gold. (11)

My foot has held fast to His steps; I have kept His way and not turned aside. (12) I have not departed from the commandment of His lips; I have treasured the words of His mouth more than my necessary food" (NKJV).

Job 30:26–28, 30, 31—"But when I looked for good, evil came to me; and when I waited for light, then came darkness. (27) My heart is in turmoil and cannot rest; days of affliction confront me. (28) I go about mourning... I stand up in the assembly and cry out for help... (30) My skin grows black and falls from me; my bones burn with fever. (31) My harp is turned to mourning, and my flute to the voice of those who weep" (NKJV).

Job 42:10–12, 16, 17—"And the Lord restored Job's losses when he prayed for his friends. Indeed the Lord gave Job twice as much as he had before. (11) Then all his brothers, all his sisters, and all those who had been his acquaintances before, came to him and ate food with him in his house; and they consoled him and comforted him for all the adversity that the Lord had brought upon him... (12) Now the Lord blessed the latter days of Job more than his beginning... (16) After this Job lived one hundred and forty years, and saw his children and grandchildren for four generations. (17) So Job died, old and full of days" (NKJV).

Philippians 1:12, 14–18—"But I want you to know, brethren, that the things which happened to me have actually turned out for the furtherance of the gospel... (14) and most of the brethren in the Lord, having become confident by my chains, are much more bold to speak the word without fear. (15) Some indeed preach Christ even from envy and strife, and some also from goodwill: (16) The former preach Christ from selfish ambition, not sincerely, supposing to add affliction to my chains; (17) but the latter out of love, knowing that I am appointed for the defense of the gospel. (18) What then? Only that in every way, whether in pretense or in truth, Christ is preached; and in this I rejoice, yes, and will rejoice" (NKJV).

God determined the end from the very beginning. Afterward, He set the ball in motion, with you and me right in the thick of it. There began our adversities. It's up to us now to discover the obvious.

Isaiah 46:9–11—"I am God, and there is none like Me, (10) declaring the end from the beginning, and from ancient times things that are not yet done, saying, 'My counsel shall stand, and I will do all My pleasure'... (11) Indeed I have spoken it; I will also bring it to pass. I have purposed it; I will also do it" (NKJV).

Everything in-between the beginning and ending, they are life's stepping stones or stumbling blocks, depending on your perspective. But after examining closely, you will find God behind the scenes, orchestrating everything. He is the Mastermind behind it all.

Pause—Listen—Reflect

* * * * * * * *

Worrisome

What seems to really aggravate us the most are the worrisome things we notice in others that we are guilty of ourselves. Nonetheless, we adamantly decree and declare that they get themselves together. But hang on just a minute. Something's terribly wrong with that picture.

We experience the very same difficulties getting ourselves together as they are challenged with getting themselves together. How can we expect of them what we do not expect of ourselves? Isn't that hypocritical? Have a drink or take a bite:

> Luke 6:41, 42—"And why beholdest thou the mote that is in thy brother's eye, but perceivest not the beam that is in thine own eye? (42) Either how canst thou say to thy brother, Brother, let me pull out the mote that is in thine eye, when thou thyself beholdest not the beam that is in thine own eye? Thou hypocrite, cast out first the beam out of thine own eye, and then shalt thou see clearly to pull out the mote that is in thy brother's eye."

Ouch! Help us, Lord, to better self-monitor instead of monitoring others. Monitoring others has become what's most worrisome to me nowadays, seeing that we are not doing much of a good job self-policing.

Pause—Listen—Reflect

* * * * * * * * *

Dominate

Let's dominate! Never allow perilous moments ushered in on you to get the upper hand. Take the lead. You are the one in command—under God, anyway. Have a drink or take a bite:

> 2 Corinthians 2:11—"After all, we don't want to unwittingly give Satan an opening for yet more mischief—we're not oblivious to his sly ways!" (MSG).

We have dominance. What else are you waiting on? Dominate!

Pause—Listen—Reflect

* * * * * * * * *

First Things First

Having all your *i*'s dotted and *t*'s crossed, checked and dou-ble-checked everything. All's good and ready to go. Let the games begin. But wait! Not so fast. Stop the train. What is this? After all the preparation we've made, how on earth did something like this happen? How did this fall apart? Someone dropped the ball. Have a drink or take a bite:

> 2 Samuel 6:2–11—"And David arose, and went with all the people that were with him from Baale of Judah, to bring up from thence the ark of God, whose name is called by the name of the Lord of hosts that dwelleth between the cherubims. (3) And they set the ark of God upon a new cart, and brought it out of the house of Abinadab that was in Gibeah: and Uzzah and Ahio, the sons of Abinadab, drave the new cart. (4) And they brought it out of the house of Abinadab which was at Gibeah, accompanying the ark of God: and Ahio went before the ark. (5) And David and all the house of Israel played before the Lord on all manner of instruments made of fir wood, even on harps, and on psalteries, and on timbrels, and on cornets, and on cymbals. (6) And when they came to Nachon's threshingfloor, Uzzah put forth his hand to the ark of God, and took hold of it; for the oxen shook it. (7) And the anger of the Lord was kindled against Uzzah; and God smote him there for his error; and there he died by the ark of God. (8) And David

was displeased, because the Lord had made a breach upon Uzzah... (9) And David was afraid of the Lord that day, and said, How shall the ark of the Lord come to me? (10) So David would not remove the ark of the Lord unto him into the city of David: but David carried it aside into the house of Obed-edom the Gittite. (11) And the ark of the Lord continued in the house of Obed-edom the Gittite three months: and the Lord blessed Obed-edom, and all his household."

1 Chronicles 15:2, 3, 11–15—"Then David said, None ought to carry the ark of God but the Levites: for them hath the Lord chosen to carry the ark of God, and to minister unto him for ever. (3) And David gathered all Israel together to Jerusalem, to bring up the ark of the Lord unto his place, which he had prepared for it... (11) And David called for Zadok and Abiathar the priests, and for the Levites... (12) And said unto them, Ye are the chief of the fathers of the Levites: sanctify yourselves, both ye and your brethren, that ye may bring up the ark of the Lord God of Israel unto the place that I have prepared for it. (13) For because ye did it not at the first, the Lord our God made a breach upon us, for that we sought him not after the due order. (14) So the priests and the Levites sanctified themselves to bring up the ark of the Lord God of Israel. (15) And the children of the Levites bare the ark of God upon their shoulders with the staves thereon, as Moses commanded according to the word of the Lord."

Lesson learned. Oh what an epiphanic moment. The moral of this story? In all your preparing, never, I mean never, never, ever forget to put first things first. Always—I mean always, no matter what—always, always seek God first before making your move.

It's invariably better to get it right the first time around so you won't have to do it over again.

It pays great dividends to follow prescribed orders. But thank God for the opportunity of a comeback; a comeback from a setback.

Pause—Listen—Reflect

* * * * * * * *

Flat Tires

Tell me, are you petrified of finishing off the last few years of life on three flat tires and the other low on air? Are you feeling 85 percent dead and 15 percent dying? Before you respond, ponder this first. Have a drink or take a bite:

> Romans 14:7–8—"For none of us liveth to himself, and no man dieth to himself. (8) For whether we live, we live unto the Lord; and whether we die, we die unto the Lord: whether we live therefore, or die, we are the Lord's."

> 2 Corinthians 1:8–10—"For we would not, brethren, have you ignorant of our trouble which came to us in Asia, that we were pressed out of measure, above strength, insomuch that we despaired even of life: (9) But we had the sentence of death in ourselves, that we should not trust in ourselves, but in God which raiseth the dead: (10) Who delivered us from so great a death, and doth deliver: in whom we trust that he will yet deliver us."

> 2 Corinthians 4:7–10—"But we have this treasure in earthen vessels, that the excellency of the power may be of God, and not of us. (8) We are troubled

on every side, yet not distressed; we are perplexed, but not in despair; (9) Persecuted, but not forsaken; cast down, but not destroyed; (10) Always bearing about in the body the dying of the Lord Jesus, that the life also of Jesus might be made manifest in our body."

2 Corinthians 5:1, 2, 4–10—"For we know that if our earthly house of this tabernacle were dissolved, we have a building of God, an house not made with hands, eternal in the heavens. (2) For in this we groan, earnestly desiring to be clothed upon with our house which is from heaven... (4) For we that are in this tabernacle do groan, being burdened: not for that we would be unclothed, but clothed upon, that mortality might be swallowed up of life. (5) Now he that hath wrought us for the selfsame thing is God, who also hath given unto us the earnest of the Spirit. (6) Therefore we are always confident, knowing that, whilst we are at home in the body, we are absent from the Lord: (7) (For we walk by faith, not by sight:) (8) We are confident, I say, and willing rather to be absent from the body, and to be present with the Lord. (9) Wherefore we labour, that, whether present or absent, we may be accepted of him. (10) For we must all appear before the judgment seat of Christ; that every one may receive the things done in his body, according to that he hath done, whether it be good or bad."

Philippians 1:20–24—"So now also Christ shall be magnified in my body, whether it be by life, or by death. (21) For to me to live is Christ, and to die is gain. (22) But if I live in the flesh, this is the fruit of my labour: yet what I shall choose I wot not. (23) For I am in a strait betwixt two, having a desire to depart, and to be with Christ; which is far better: (24) Nevertheless to abide in the flesh is more needful for you."

2 Timothy 4:6–8—"For I am now ready to be offered, and the time of my departure is at hand. (7) I have fought a good fight, I have finished my course, I have kept the faith: (8) Henceforth there is laid up for me a crown of righteousness, which the Lord, the righteous judge, shall give me at that day: and not to me only, but unto all them also that love his appearing."

We all experience feeling a little flat at times on our way out, but a mighty rushing wind is blowing, strong enough to inflate any flats. Live well so you may end well. Then, when it's time, you will die well, but not one second before your appointed time.

Pause—Listen—Reflect

* * * * * * * * *

Get Dressed

Get dressed. It's all right. Go ahead. Try it on. If it fits, wear it. It will look fabulous on you. If it doesn't, well, let's see. Have a drink or take a bite:

Job 29:14—"I put on righteousness, and it clothed me: My judgment was as a robe and a diadem."

Isaiah 59:17—"For he put on righteousness as a breastplate, and an helmet of salvation upon his head; and he put on the garments of vengeance for clothing, and was clad with zeal as a cloke."

Isaiah 61:10—"I will greatly rejoice in the Lord, my soul shall be joyful in my God; for he hath clothed me with the garments of salvation, he hath covered me with the robe of righteousness, as a bridegroom decketh himself with ornaments, and as a bride adorneth herself with her jewels."

Romans 13:14—"But put ye on the Lord Jesus Christ, and make not provision for the flesh, to fulfil the lusts thereof."

Ephesians 4:24—"And that ye put on the new man, which after God is created in righteousness and true holiness."

Ephesians 6:11–17—"Put on the whole armour of God, that ye may be able to stand against the wiles of the devil. (12) For we wrestle not against flesh and blood, but against principalities, against powers, against the rulers of the darkness of this world, against spiritual wickedness in high places. (13) Wherefore take unto you the whole armour of God, that ye may be able to withstand in the evil day, and having done all, to stand. (14) Stand therefore, having your loins girt about with truth, and having on the breastplate of righteousness; (15) And your feet shod with the preparation of the gospel of peace; (16) Above all, taking the shield of faith, wherewith ye shall be able to quench all the fiery darts of the wicked. (17) And take the helmet of salvation, and the sword of the Spirit, which is the word of God."

Colossians 3:10, 12—"And have put on the new man, which is renewed in knowledge after the image of him that created him... (12) Put on therefore, as the elect of God, holy and beloved, bowels

of mercies, kindness, humbleness of mind, meek-
ness, longsuffering..."

Well, here it is. If it doesn't fit, put off the disposables, so that it
will. One thing for sure: you definitely do not look attractive running around nearly naked. Take it from the rest of us. You are not
a pretty sight half-dressed. Well, maybe a very pretty ugly sight.

Pause—Listen—Reflect

* * * * * * * *

Nearly Impossible

It seems nearly impossible to make a comeback from this, you all.
I have never seen anything as utterly despairing as this. I don't
know. It will take nothing short of a miracle to resurrect this, for
sure. Have a drink or take a bite:

> Ezekiel 37:1–3, 5, 7–10—"The hand of the Lord
> was upon me, and carried me out in the spirit of the
> Lord, and set me down in the midst of the valley
> which was full of bones, (2) And caused me to
> pass by them round about: and, behold, there were
> very many in the open valley; and, lo, they were
> very dry. (3) And he said unto me, Son of man, can
> these bones live? And I answered, O Lord God,
> thou knowest... (5) Thus saith the Lord God unto
> these bones; Behold, I will cause breath to enter
> into you, and ye shall live... (7) So I prophesied
> as I was commanded: and as I prophesied, there
> was a noise, and behold a shaking, and the bones
> came together, bone to his bone. (8) And when I
> beheld, lo, the sinews and the flesh came up upon
> them, and the skin covered them above: but there
> was no breath in them. (9) Then said he unto me,

Prophesy unto the wind, prophesy, son of man, and say to the wind, Thus saith the Lord God; Come from the four winds, O breath, and breathe upon these slain, that they may live. (10) So I prophesied as he commanded me, and the breath came into them, and they lived, and stood up upon their feet, an exceeding great army."

John 11:21, 23, 25, 34, 39, 43, 44—"Then said Martha unto Jesus, Lord, if thou hadst been here, my brother had not died... (23) Jesus saith unto her, Thy brother shall rise again... (25) Jesus said unto her, I am the resurrection, and the life: he that believeth in me, though he were dead, yet shall he live... (34) And said, Where have ye laid him? They said unto him, Lord, come and see... (39) Jesus said, Take ye away the stone. Martha, the sister of him that was dead, saith unto him, Lord, by this time he stinketh: for he hath been dead four days... (43) And when he thus had spoken, he cried with a loud voice, Lazarus, come forth (44) And he that was dead came forth, bound hand and foot with graveclothes: and his face was bound about with a napkin. Jesus saith unto them, Loose him, and let him go."

I can hear the rumbling sound as of a mighty rushing wind. And it sounds like a life-giving sound at that. Not all things dead are fitting to be buried. Some things are destined to be resurrected. Do you hear what I hear? Ladies and gentlemen, let's get ready to rrrrumble!

Pause—Listen—Reflect

* * * * * * * *

What's Cooking?

What have you got cooking up over there? Whatever it is, I assure you, it's nothing half as incredibly delicious, succulent, mouthwatering, appetizing, or tasty as what's brewing over here. Have a drink or take a bite:

> Exodus 16:4, 13–15, 31—"Then said the Lord unto Moses, Behold, I will rain bread from heaven for you; and the people shall go out and gather a certain rate every day... (13) And it came to pass, that at even the quails came up, and covered the camp: and in the morning the dew lay round about the host. (14) And when the dew that lay was gone up, behold, upon the face of the wilderness there lay a small round thing, as small as the hoar frost on the ground. (15) And when the children of Israel saw it, they said one to another, It is manna: for they wist not what it was. And Moses said unto them, This is the bread which the Lord hath given you to eat... (31) And the house of Israel called the name thereof Manna: and it was like coriander seed, white; and the taste of it was like wafers made with honey."

> Deuteronomy 8:3—"And he humbled thee, and suffered thee to hunger, and fed thee with manna, which thou knewest not, neither did thy fathers know; that he might make thee know that man doth not live by bread only, but by every word that proceedeth out of the mouth of the Lord doth man live."

> John 6:31–33, 35, 48–51, 53–58—"Our fathers did eat manna in the desert; as it is written, He gave them bread from heaven to eat. (32) Then Jesus said unto them, Verily, verily, I say unto you,

147

Moses gave you not that bread from heaven; but
my Father giveth you the true bread from heaven.
(33) For the bread of God is he which cometh
down from heaven, and giveth life unto the world...
(35) And Jesus said unto them, I am the bread of
life: he that cometh to me shall never hunger; and
he that believeth on me shall never thirst... (48)
I am that bread of life. (49) Your fathers did eat
manna in the wilderness, and are dead. (50) This
is the bread which cometh down from heaven, that
a man may eat thereof, and not die. (51) I am the
living bread which came down from heaven: if any
man eat of this bread, he shall live for ever: and
the bread that I will give is my flesh, which I will
give for the life of the world... (53) Then Jesus said
unto them, Verily, verily, I say unto you, Except
ye eat the flesh of the Son of man, and drink his
blood, ye have no life in you. (54) Whoso eateth
my flesh, and drinketh my blood, hath eternal life;
and I will raise him up at the last day. (55) For
my flesh is meat indeed, and my blood is drink
indeed. (56) He that eateth my flesh, and drinketh
my blood, dwelleth in me, and I in him. (57)... so
he that eateth me, even he shall live by me. (58)
This is that bread which came down from heaven:
not as your fathers did eat manna, and are dead: he
that eateth of this bread shall live for ever."

1 Corinthians 10:3, 4—"And did all eat the same
spiritual meat; (4) And did all drink the same spiritual drink: for they drank of that spiritual Rock that
followed them: and that Rock was Christ."

This bread from heaven, it's better than angel's food. It truly is
meat indeed. The Master Chef's on duty, serving up the Bread of
Life; serving it up on a platter. There's absolutely no competition,

hands down. Pull up and take a seat at the Lord's table. Feel free to partake of this Holy Communion.

Pause—Listen—Reflect

* * * * * * * * *

What's Going On?

At one moment, it's as if we are on top of the world. Then in the very next moment, what seems like in the blink of an eye, we're suddenly thrown right back down again. Can a brother or sister catch a break? We asked for no more than the next man. They appear to be thriving while we're barely surviving. What in the world is going on here? Something about this pattern just isn't right or fair. Have a drink or take a bite:

> Job 1:7, 8—"And the Lord said unto Satan, Whence comest thou? Then Satan answered the Lord, and said, From going to and fro in the earth, and from walking up and down in it. (8) And the Lord said unto Satan, Hast thou considered my servant Job, that there is none like him in the earth, a perfect and an upright man, one that feareth God, and escheweth evil?"

> Luke 22:31, 32—"And the Lord said, Simon, Simon, behold, Satan hath desired to have you, that he may sift you as wheat: (32) But I have prayed for thee, that thy faith fail not: and when thou art converted, strengthen thy brethren."

> 1 Corinthians 10:12—"Wherefore let him that thinketh he standeth take heed lest he fall."

2 Corinthians 2:11—"Lest Satan should get an advantage of us: for we are not ignorant of his devices."

Ephesians 6:11–14, 17, 18—"Put on the whole armour of God, that ye may be able to stand against the wiles of the devil. (12) For we wrestle not against flesh and blood, but against principalities, against powers, against the rulers of the darkness of this world, against spiritual wickedness in high places. (13) Wherefore take unto you the whole armour of God, that ye may be able to withstand in the evil day, and having done all, to stand. (14) Stand therefore... (17) And take the helmet of salvation, and the sword of the Spirit, which is the word of God: (18) Praying always with all prayer and supplication in the Spirit, and watching thereunto with all perseverance and supplication for all saints."

1 Peter 1:13—"Wherefore gird up the loins of your mind, be sober, and hope to the end for the grace that is to be brought unto you at the revelation of Jesus Christ."

1 Peter 5:8—"Be sober, be vigilant; because your adversary the devil, as a roaring lion, walketh about, seeking whom he may devour."

2 Peter 3:17—"Ye therefore, beloved, seeing ye know these things before, beware lest ye also, being led away with the error of the wicked, fall from your own stedfastness."

Revelation 12:11—"And they overcame him by the blood of the Lamb, and by the word of their testimony; and they loved not their lives unto the death."

Oh, all right. I see. He's the one behind this. So we are not losing it after all. Satan, you are a liar, a thief, and a robber. A defeated foe, you are. You loser! You are fighting a losing battle. You cannot win. It's a fixed fight. That is what's going on. In the end, we win!

Pause—Listen—Reflect

Conclusion

I can think of no better note on which to bring this book to a close than to say we take serious matters seriously. By far, our spiritual growth, development, and maturity depend entirely on the diet we subscribe to. Specifically, toddlers require a consistent diet of milk, which is vital for developing strong bones and teeth and enhances muscle growth. Children who are deprived of this form of nourishment eventually grow to display certain forms of malnourishment and deformity. It is all but impossible for those children to entirely recover from such maladies later in life.

Conversely, infants who receive a steady diet of milk throughout their younger years go on to develop stronger, healthier, and much more able bodies that begin to crave stronger foods in their diets, namely strong meat. At a certain stage in the growth process, milk becomes insufficient for the sustenance of growing toddlers on their way into adulthood. Although milk played the primary role in the babe's early diet, as its body grows, it desperately yearns for something more, something much more efficient to facilitate its growing expanse.

This craving alone underlines the fact that milk is an utmost necessity for young growing babes. Without it, they will soon display some forms of physical handicaps. As they continue on their journey to becoming grown-ups, their growing appetite for strong meat bursts on the scene and makes its presence known. Once strong meat becomes a part of their necessary diet, the young adults begin to exercise themselves in their newly forming, developing, maturing, growing, and grown-up bodies.

Oh, what joy and jubilation this sight brings to the parents looking on as their once-young babes begin transitioning into lively, growing, maturing grown-ups. I have described the natural growth, development, and maturing process of the physical body of children becoming adults. From what you have read in this book so far, my hope is that, beyond the natural and physical, what primarily shone through all that I have written is the overwhelming certainty that milk is for babes while strong meat belongs to grown-ups. Therefore:

> Philippians 2:12—"Work out your own salvation with fear and trembling."

> 2 Peter 1:10—"Give diligence to make your calling and election sure: for if ye do these things, ye shall never fall."

This is a seriously critical and consequential matter. Take serious matters seriously.

One final task: if your eyes have landed on this paragraph as my writing draws near its climax, and you find yourself unsure of where you stand as it pertains to your relationship with the Lord Jesus Christ, or you simply have never invited Him into your heart and life, here's what I invite you to do right this very moment. First, confess that you were conceived and born in sin, according to Psalm 51:5—"For I was born a sinner—yes, from the moment my mother conceived me" (NLT). Second, invite Jesus into your heart and life and believe that He hears and answers your request the very moment you pray. These are the instructions we're given in Romans 10:9, 10—"If you openly declare that Jesus is Lord and believe in your heart that God raised Him from the dead, you will be saved. (10) For it is by believing in your heart that you are made right with God, and it is by openly declaring your faith that you are saved" (NLT). Do not be cheated out of sharing your personal salvation testimony with the very first person you make contact with immediately after you finish this prayer.

Finally, pray and ask God to lead you to a local assembly that preaches and teaches the Truth as it is found in the holy Scriptures. Hebrews 10:25 encourages disciples of the Lord Jesus Christ to "not avoiding worshiping together as some do but spurring each other on, especially as we see the big Day approaching" (MSG).

If you have prayed along these lines and believe in your heart that God heard and answered your prayer, *congratulations*, you are now a newborn babe in Christ Jesus. As a natural newborn desires milk, so, too, the spiritual newborn craves the pure milk of God's Word (1 Pet. 2:2). Once you have started on this journey, you are well on your way from being a newborn babe in Christ to becoming a fully-grown grown-up. Soon, you will be able to digest the strong meat of God's Word. I decree and declare our Lord's unmerited favor upon your life from this moment forward, even for evermore. Amen!

Welcome to the family of Christ.

About The Author

Raul N. Wallace hails from Manchester, Jamaica. He migrated to Hartford, Connecticut, in the USA at nine years of age. Raul graduated from Hartford Public High School in 1982, then went on to serve in the United States Air Force for twenty-five years. He retired from active military service in 2010 and currently resides in Fayetteville, North Carolina.

Raul Wallace received his ministry ordination as an elder in 1994. He formerly served nine years as assistant pastor of Kingdom Impact Global Ministries in Fayetteville, North Carolina. Raul is a graduate of Methodist University with a bachelor of science degree in clinical/counseling psychology. He also holds an associate's in applied science from the Community College of the Air Force.

His military achievements and awards include distinguished graduate USAF Senior NCO Academy, John Levitow Award recipient, Air Force Meritorious Service Medal (3 OLC), Air Force Commendation Medal (2 OLC), Air Force Achievement Medal, Southwest Asia Service Medal, Kuwait Liberation Medal Kingdom of Saudi Arabia, and Kuwait Liberation Medal Government of Kuwait. During his military career, besides serving within the United States, he was stationed in Italy and Turkey as well as deployed to southwest Asia in support of Operations Desert Shield/Desert Storm, Enduring Freedom, and Iraqi Freedom.

Those who know the author best are very familiar with his life's motto: "All is well and getting better." Raul N. Wallace is happily married to the former Juanetta Solomon since June 1988.

To contact the author, you may connect with him via email at raul.wallace@icloud.com or on Facebook at www.facebook.com/raul.wallace.583

CPSIA information can be obtained
at www.ICGtesting.com
Printed in the USA
LVHW050035160321
681579LV00018B/178